Jenkins Brothers of Cardiff:

A Ceredigion Family's Shipping Ventures

Jenkins Brothers of Cardiff:
A Ceredigion Family's Shipping Ventures

by David Jenkins

Amgueddfa Genedlaethol Cymru
National Museum of Wales
Caerdydd/Cardiff 1985

Other titles in the series are:

Morels of Cardiff: the History of a Family Shipping Firm.
By John Morel Gibbs. 1982

Evan Thomas Radcliffe, a Cardiff Shipowning Company.
By J. Geraint Jenkins. 1982

© National Museum of Wales
First Published 1985
Production: Hywel Gealy Rees
Design: Cloud Nine Design
Typesetting: Afal, Cardiff
Type: 10pt. Garamond
Paper: Matt Art 135gsm.
Printing: South Western Printers, Caerphilly

ISBN: 0 7200 0296 6

Contents

In memory of my great-grandfather,
Captain David Jenkins *(Morfab)*
1857-1911

Master of the steamships
Straits of Menai, Italiana, Farringford and *Cardigan*

Foreword

During the last quarter of the nineteenth century Cardiff developed into one of the great ports of the world and its wealth was based almost entirely on the export of coal to all quarters of the globe. The great commercial activity in the port attracted shipowners from many other parts of Britain and the European continent who came to Cardiff in search of a fortune. Although some of the old-established Cardiff families that owned fleets of sailing vessels invested in new steam-ships for the coal trade, the lead was provided by immigrant businessmen who made Cardiff the principal tramp-steamer owning port in the Kingdom. They came from the West of England, from the Channel Islands, from Tyneside and Scandinavia; a few came from the rural areas of West and North Wales.

A West Wales village that provided Cardiff with four important shipping ventures was the Ceredigion coastal settlement of Aber-porth, long famed as a centre of herring fishing and coastal trading. The history of one of those Cardiff companies that originated in Aber-porth was the subject of the second book in the series, *Evan Thomas Radcliffe, a Cardiff Shipowning Company.* Captain Evan Thomas of Dôl-wen, Aber-porth, founded one of the largest of all Cardiff shipping companies in association with Henry Radcliffe of Merthyr Tudful in 1882. The company of Jenkins Bros. of Cardiff, the subject of this third volume in the series, was founded in 1897 by an Aber-porth master mariner who, for some years, served on the tramp vessels of Evan Thomas Radcliffe & Co. This book was written by David Jenkins, Research Assistant at the Welsh Industrial and Maritime Museum, whose great-grandfather too, was an Aber-porth master mariner and was, for some years, master of vessels owned by the Jenkins Bros.

J. Geraint Jenkins,
Curator,
Welsh Industrial and Maritime Museum

Acknowledgements

This book may be said to have its origins in some notes jotted down by my father in August 1970 while in conversation with my late great-uncle, Captain Samuel Jenkins, 'Clydfan', Aber-porth. They were discussing the career of my great-grandfather, Captain David Jenkins, who died at Buenos Aires in January 1911 while in command of the S.S. *Cardigan*, one of the tramp steamers owned by Jenkins Bros. of Cardiff. Though not related to the family with whose shipping ventures this book is concerned, my own forefathers in Aber-porth (like many another family in the village) were heavily dependant upon the locally-founded company for employment. With the collective experience of a century and a half of seafaring in the village – and being themselves natives of Aber-porth – it was only natural that Jenkins Bros. should employ local mariners on their vessels. One such mariner was *'Wncwl Sam, Clydfan'* and my first thanks must go to him for recalling something of Aber-porth's rich maritime heritage and to my father for recording his reminiscences.

Research work in preparation for the exhibition 'The Maritime Heritage of Dyfed', staged at the Welsh Industrial and Maritime Museum in December 1982, revealed many interesting photographs and much useful information relating to the history of Jenkins Bros. and it was the Curator, Dr. Geraint Jenkins, who suggested that I might extend my research to see whether there was enough material available to write this book. I am deeply grateful to him for his constant encouragement and constructive criticisms. I owe an inestimable debt to Mr. Robin Craig, formerly of University College, London who shared with a mere novice like myself his unrivalled knowledge of merchant shipping in general and tramp steamers in particular. Without his generous help, this book could not have been contemplated. Thanks are also due to Mr. David Jenkins of the University College of Wales, Aberystwyth, on whose expert knowledge of the society of West Wales at the turn of the century I have relied heavily and Mr. Harold Appleyard and his colleagues in the World Ship Society who provided detailed histories of the companies' tramp steamers.

The bulk of documentary material relating to the history of Jenkins Bros. was apparently destroyed in a bomb attack on Cardiff docks during the Second World War. I have had to rely heavily, therefore, on the assistance of numerous individuals (many of whom were in some way associated with the firm) and also upon material preserved in various archives and libraries, chiefly in Cardiff and London. I am particularly indebted to the following persons for their invaluable aid: Dr. Roderic Bowen, Cardiff, Mr. David Burrell, Sevenoaks, Mr. Frank Chagnon, Aber-porth, Mr. and Mrs. A. Davies, Aber-porth, Mr. D.V.T. Davies, Cardigan, Miss I. Davies, Radyr, Mr. Aled Eames, Moelfre, Mrs. H. Evans, Radyr, Mr. J.M. Griffith, Rhoslan, Mrs. D. Hemming,

Cardiff, Captain and Mrs. Daniel Jenkins, Swansea, Mr. and Mrs. D.B. Jenkins, Wraysbury, Middlesex, Miss E.E. Jenkins, Aber-porth, Mrs. M. Jenkins, Aberystwyth, Dr. O.C. Jenkins, Menai Bridge, Captain Roy Jenkins, Aber-porth, Mrs. N. John, Aber-porth, Mr. K. Maitland-Davies, London, Mrs. M. Mathias, Tre-saith, Mr. R.C.B. Oliver, Llandrindod Wells, Mrs. C. Redmore, Backwell, Bristol, Mr. C.A. Roberts, Little Maplestead, Essex, Mr. E.J. Roberts, Sully, Mrs. N. Thomas, Ludlow and Mr. H. Walters, Aberystwyth.

I wish to thank members of staff of the following bodies: The British Library (Newspaper division, Colindale) London, Cardiff Central Reference Library, Companies' House, Cardiff, Dyfed Archives, Haverfordwest, Glamorgan Archive Service, Cardiff, Guildhall Library, London, H.M. Customs and Excise, Fishguard, Cardiff and London, Hartlepool Maritime Museum, Maritime History Group of the Memorial University of Newfoundland, Canada, National Library of Wales, Aberystwyth, National Maritime Museum, Greenwich, London, Science Museum, Newcastle-upon-Tyne and the World Ship Society.

Messrs. T.G. Evans and James Lawson helped me to unravel the intricacies of balance sheets and my colleagues Bill Jones, Don Taylor and Tom Sharpe also assisted me with information on certain topics in which they specialise. Most of the plates in the book are from negatives in the Museum's photographic archive and I am indebted to the staff of the photographic department at Cathays Park for their assistance; photographs other than those from the museum's archive are individually acknowledged. The entire book has been typed by Mrs. Carolyn Greene, while Miss Marian Owen also typed some early drafts. I am deeply grateful to everyone who has been of assistance. *Diolch yn fawr iawn i bawb.*

David Jenkins,
Research Assistant,
Welsh Industrial and Maritime Museum

Introduction

The village of Aber-porth on the coastline of Ceredigion has a long and fascinating tradition of maritime associations. It was formerly one of the foremost herring fishing centres in Wales, while during the nineteenth century, the farmers and merchants of the area were the joint owners of a fleet of some twenty locally-manned trading smacks and ketches that supplied the village and its hinterland with virtually all their fuel and fertilizers. With the coming of the railway to Ceredigion, this local trade declined and from the 1880s onwards many mariners from the area found employment in the growing fleet of tramp steamers that exported the 'black gold' of South Wales from Cardiff to all parts of the world.

It is a remarkable fact that no fewer than four tramp shipping companies set up in Cardiff around the turn of the century were founded by master mariners from Aber-porth, often in association with South Walian businessmen; few other villages in Wales can boast such a concentration of entrepreneurialism at that time. The first of these was Evan Thomas, Radcliffe & Co., founded in 1882 by Evan Thomas of Aber-porth and Henry Radcliffe of Merthyr Tudful, a company which was to become one of the best-known of all British tramp shipping concerns. Fifteen years later, in 1897, the company which eventually became known as Jenkins Bros. was established in Cardiff by James Jenkins of Fron-dêg, Aber-porth, later joined by his brother-in-law, David. Their family had been involved in the local coasting trade of Ceredigion since the 1860s, but moved into Cardiff tramp shipping around the turn of the century. A third member of the family, Daniel, set up as a ship-owner in Cardiff in 1903, though his shipping venture, (like that of the fourth Aber-porth-founded tramp shipping company set up in the same year by Captain Thomas Owen) was to prove relatively short-lived. The company founded by James Jenkins, however, continued to trade until its founder's retirement in 1927 and during the intervening thirty years, participated successfully in the keenly competitive tramp shipping market.

This book is an attempt to relate the history of the companies founded by members of the Jenkins family in Cardiff around the turn of the century, both from the point of view of Cardiff's shipping industry, then in its prime, and the maritime communities of Ceredigion and other parts of Wales whose menfolk earned a living in the tough and uncompromising conditions on board the tramp steamers of the time.

CHAPTER 1

The *Mary Jane* and the *James*

The coastline of Ceredigion can boast a deeply entrenched tradition of seafaring and maritime activity dating back to prehistoric times. Until the coming of the railway to the area during the latter half of the nineteenth century it was a relatively isolated corner of Wales, though to the inhabitants the sea was both a bountiful larder and a highway whereby those necessities of life not available in the area could be imported. The pace of maritime activity in the area quickened considerably from the 1760s onwards and by the mid-nineteenth century the seafaring associations of Ceredigion's coastal communities had achieved a zenith. The sea provided a plentiful source of food, particularly the herring that congregated in vast shaols off the coast each autumn, while by 1850 each community could boast its fleet of sailing coasters, actively engaged upon the import of coal, culm, lime and the general merchandise required by the coastal communities and their hinterland.

One such community was Aber-porth, some six miles north-east of Cardigan. Together with Nefyn in the Llŷn Peninsula it was one of Wales's most important herring fishing ports and from September until Christmas each year the

A general view of Aber-porth at the turn of the century

catching of herring pre-occupied the menfolk of the village.[1] Originally the herring, salted or pickled in barrels, had also been an important export, but it was the import of various staple commodities that predominated by the mid-nineteenth century. The main imports were culm and coal from Hook, Saundersfoot, Llanelli, Swansea and Cardiff, limestone from south Pembrokeshire, slates from Porthmadog and Caernarfon and general building materials from a variety of sources.

The vessels that developed to handle this trade were simple and practical bulk carriers. They generally had to discharge their cargoes on open beaches at low tide and were built with flat-bottomed hulls that enabled them to stand upright on dry sands. The fact that they often had to sail in narrow and shallow channels limited their size and tonnage and there was, therefore, no need for extensive and complicated rigging. Thus the coasting trade of Ceredigion in its heyday was handled largely by single-masted, fore and aft rigged vessels with full, flat-bottomed hulls known as smacks or sloops. Rarely of more than fifty gross tons and generally crewed by two men and a boy, there were over twenty such vessels owned in the Aber-porth area alone in 1840.[2] According to the legislation of 1824, each vessel was divided into sixty-four shares and these were held by consortiums made up of farmers, merchants, craftsmen and some seamen, being those people most involved in the trade of the vessels.

One such vessel was the *Mary Jane,* a smack of thirty gross tons completed by John Williams of Netpool, Cardigan in 1868. Williams was a well-known shipwright who built a large number of coastal sailing vessels at his Cardigan yard from the 1840s onwards and his was one of half a dozen shipyards operating in the Cardigan area at that time.[3] The *Mary Jane* was built to the order of a consortium headed by Griffith Jenkins, Dyffryn Mill *(Y Felin),* Aber-porth. Griffith Jenkins was typical of the small rural entrepreneurs who invested in the coastal shipping of Ceredigion at that time; in an 1878 list of the directors of the 'Aberporth Mutual Ship Insurance Society', (of which he was a founder member), he described himself as 'merchant and shipowner'[4] and he was the major shareholder and managing owner of the new smack. The initial shareholders and their shares in the *Mary Jane* were:

Griffith Jenkins of Aber-porth, managing owner	33 shares
D.G. Davies of Cardigan, merchant	2 shares
Laurence Lowther of Cardigan, merchant	2 shares
John Davies of Aber-porth, master mariner	1 share
Daniel Jenkins of Aber-porth, mariner	6 shares
David Jones of Tre-saith, farmer	4 shares
Lewis Jones of Cardigan, sailmaker	4 shares
John Parry of Llangrannog, blacksmith	2 shares
David Thomas of Blaen-porth, farm servant	2 shares
Eliza Lowther of Bradford, spinster	4 shares
John Thomas of Cardiff, shipbroker	4 shares
	64 5

In addition to his shipping interests Griffith Jenkins was also the owner of a small holding and mill that stood on the banks of the Howni brook a quarter of a mile from *Traeth y Llongau* – the Ship Beach – where the Howni meets the sea. It was to this beach that Griffith Jenkins' smack, named after his wife, was to trade regularly during the latter decades of the nineteenth century.

Four coastal trading smacks beached at Traeth y Llongau, *Aber-porth, c.1890. The second vessel from the right is Griffith Jenkins's smack,* Mary Jane

Griffith Jenkins was the sailing master as well as the owner of the *Mary Jane* and he left Cardigan on the new vessel's maiden voyage in March 1868, bound for Caernarfon in ballast.[6] His crew consisted of his younger brother Daniel (one of the shareholders) as mate and Thomas Davies as deck boy. Both were natives of Aber-porth; indeed it was almost invariably the case that these little vessels were manned by men from the villages where they were owned. At Caernarfon the *Mary Jane* took on a cargo of slates for Cardiff and on the 11 May she left Cardiff for Milford Haven with a cargo of steam coal. She eventually got back to Cardigan late in May with a cargo of limestone from Lydstep before sailing in ballast to Llanelli to load a cargo of culm. This was typical of the pattern of trading in which these sailing coasters participated. The *Mary Jane* also visited Aber-porth regularly; during the months of July and August 1878, for instance, she was at her home port on four occasions, twice with cargoes of limestone from south Pembrokeshire and twice with cargoes of culm from Swansea and Burry

Port. That year also saw a slight change in the composition of the crew when David, Griffith Jenkins's eldest son, joined the vessel as mate in place of his uncle, Daniel.

During the 1870s, Griffith Jenkins pursued a policy of buying up shares in the *Mary Jane* held by other shareholders. By 1879 he held fifty-two shares in the vessel, while eight other shares were held by his brothers John and Daniel. John Jenkins had not been among the original shareholders, but in 1869 he had purchased the shares of Eliza Lowther, thus giving the Jenkins family what amounted to total control of the vessel. In 1882, however, John ventured into shipowning on his own account when he purchased the *James,* a smack of thirty-five gross tons completed at Cardigan in 1864 at the same shipyard as the *Mary Jane.* The *James* was built originally to the order of David Davies of Aber-porth, master mariner, though a third of the shares were held initially by William Stephens of Llechryd who owned the slate quarries at Cilgerran, some three miles up the Teifi from Cardigan. In February 1873, following the death of William Stephens, his son John bought the vessel outright and the *James* joined the fleet of four schooners and a brigantine already owned by Stephens to distribute the produce of the quarries.[7]

The Jenkins Family

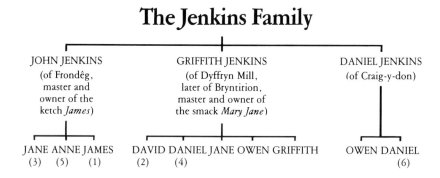

JOHN JENKINS
(of Frondêg,
master and
owner of the
ketch *James*)

GRIFFITH JENKINS
(of Dyffryn Mill,
later of Bryntirion,
master and owner of
the smack *Mary Jane*)

DANIEL JENKINS
(of Craig-y-don)

JANE ANNE JAMES
(3)   (5)   (1)

DAVID DANIEL JANE OWEN GRIFFITH
(2)   (4)

OWEN DANIEL
(6)

James (1) of Frondêg entered into shipping in Cardiff in 1896-97, later in partnership with W.J. Williams of Bethesda. In 1904 this partnership was ended and James went into partnership with his cousin David (2) of Bryntirion to form Jenkins Bros. The partners were brothers-in-law by virtue of the fact that David had married his cousin Jane (3) of Frondêg, James' sister.

Daniel (4) of Bryntirion ventured into shipowning in 1903 by buying the ex-Radcliffe vessel S.S.*W.I.Radcliffe* (which was re-named S.S.*Aberporth*) and setting up the Aberporth Steamship Co. Ltd.

Anne (5) of Frondêg owned and operated her father's ketch *James* until 1929.

Daniel (6) of Craig-y-don, later of Brynberwyn, Tre-saith, commanded a number of his cousins' vessels between 1902 and 1907.

John Jenkins purchased all sixty-four shares in the *James* on 2 February 1882, and having given sixteen shares each to his daughters Jane and Anne, proceeded to operate the smack as master and managing owner, bringing cargoes of coal, culm, lime and slate to Aber-porth and the adjacent coastal villages. He also retained his shares in the *Mary Jane,* which, in 1892, came to be owned entirely by members of the Jenkins family, with Griffith Jenkins holding fifty-eight of the sixty-four shares. By that date, Griffith Jenkins was almost sixty years old and would appear to have retired from active sea-faring, for he had begun to employ a master – Samuel Jones, New Terrace, Aber-porth – to sail the vessel. Griffith Jenkins had also left Dyffryn Mill and moved to a newly-built house called Bryntirion. During the last twenty years of the nineteenth century, the small surplus of wealth that gradually had been amassed in Aber-porth over many decades of sea trading eventually began to take on a material expression as the village began to expand beyond the confines of a cluster of cottages on the seashore and in the narrow valley of the Howni.[8] Bryntirion was one of a row of new houses constructed on the fields above the old village and many of these houses were the homes of ship owners and more prosperous master mariners.

Fron-dêg, Aber-porth, the birthplace of James Jenkins. It is now the Highcliffe Hotel. (Mr. Alun Davies, Aber-porth)

15

John Jenkins, too, retired from active seafaring in the early 1890s and in May 1893, handed over most of his shares in the *James* to his daughter Anne. Soon afterwards Miss Jenkins withdrew the vessel from active trading and the *James* returned to Cardigan to undergo a thorough re-building, during which she was re-rigged as a ketch. A number of smacks were re-rigged in this way in the 1890s, a ketch rig with its mizzen mast and sail being far handier than the long heavy boom and massive mainsail of the smacks.[9] Classified A1 by Lloyd's surveyors in November 1895, the *James* then returned to the sea under her new master, David Evans of Tŷ Mawr, Aber-porth, together with a crew of two Aber-porth mariners. The *Mary Jane* was never re-rigged in this way, however; she foundered and sank on St. Patrick's Causeway on 7 March 1894, bringing to an end over a quarter of a century's shipowning by Griffith Jenkins.

The loss of the *Mary Jane* signalled the end of an era in more than one way, for the pattern of trade was changing as the expanding railway system extended its tentacles to West Wales in the 1890s, depriving the coastal ports of their natural hinterland. Local ship owners were forced to employ their vessels on trades that rarely brought them to their home ports and this was certainly true of the *James*. Throughout 1896, for instance, she did not call once at Aber-porth and she docked only once in a Ceredigion port with a cargo of coal from Cardiff to Aberaeron. Otherwise she was intensively employed tramping coal from various South Wales ports to Porthmadog or Caernarfon and returning to South Wales with slates.[10] Indeed, for a short period during that year the *James* was registered as being managed by John Jenkins's son James, not at Aber-porth but at 129 Bute Street, Cardiff. James had retired from active sea-faring in January 1896, having been master of the S.S.*Regnant* of Liverpool and he had moved to Cardiff probably because it was easier to obtain charters for the little ketch in the booming coal port. Her pattern of trading, furthermore, suggests that she was being operated more as a Cardiff coasting collier than a Ceredigion coaster at that time. Within a year, however, James Jenkins had ventured into steam tramp ownership and the *James* reverted to her former Aber-porth ownership.

By the first decade of the twentieth century the coastal trade of Ceredigion had entered upon a period of terminal decline. Nevertheless, Miss Anne Jenkins continued to operate the ketch and on those occasions that the *James* visited Aber-porth, the vessel is remembered by the village's older inhabitants for her immaculate appearance. Miss Jenkins occasionally sailed on the *James* herself as 'business master' and was apparently quite competent in navigation though she possessed no formal sea-going qualifications.[11] The *James* continued to ply chiefly between the coal ports of South Wales and the slate harbours of Gwynedd, calling only rarely at any of the Ceredigion ports, but even then cargoes were not always available and the little ketch was laid up at Cardigan from October 1908 until June 1910.

*A typical coastal trading ketch awaiting the tide at the Netpool, Cardigan.
The* James *was laid up here from October 1908 until June 1910.
(Mr. D.V.T. Davies, Cardigan)*

By 1910 there was a wide variety of berths available to the mariners of Ceredigion in the world-wide tramping trades out of Cardiff and other British ports. Fewer sailors wished to man the little sailing coasters and many of their owners were being forced to sell up as fewer suitable cargoes became available for their vessels. The instability of the trade was to some degree reflected in the manning of the *James* at that time. Old masters and young boys made up the crew of the vessel in the early 1900s and they were not exclusively Aber-porth men, but a mixture of men from coastal communities all over Wales and further afield. The most unusual was a certain John Donohue, a native of Massachusetts, who served on board the *James* during the first six months of 1906. He had previously served on board the well-known Aberystwyth schooner, *Aeron Belle,* though what had brought him from America to serve on vessels such as these remains a mystery.

By the 1920s the age of the locally-owned and locally-manned Ceredigion sailing coasters was practically over; the last time that a merchant vessel visited Aber-porth was probably in the mid-nineteen twenties.[12] Miss Anne Jenkins, however, continued to operate the *James* until 1929. It is not clear what happened to the vessel after this date, but a note among her crew agreements records the fact that she was not declared unseaworthy until 13 August 1937. By this date, Anne Jenkins's brother, James, had long since ceased his involvement in Cardiff tramp shipping and it is ironic to think that the *James,* built in 1864, was still in the hands of a member of the Jenkins family after they had disposed of the last of their modern tramp steamers in March 1927. Had it not been for a phenomenal development of the South Wales coalfield in the latter half of the nineteenth century, this chapter probably would have sufficed to relate the entire story of the Jenkins family and their shipping interests. There was, however, a fortune to be made in the exporting of coal from Cardiff's Bute Docks to all parts of the world and James Jenkins was one of the many ambitious entrepreneurs who moved from all parts of the British Isles and further afield in the late nineteenth century to take advantage of these opportunities.

CHAPTER 2

The Move to Cardiff

With the development of the railway system in South-West Wales during the later decades of the nineteenth century, the trade of Ceredigion's ports entered upon a period of gradual, but inexorable, decline and the berths available to local sailors on board the smacks and ketches of the coastal trade decreased accordingly. Nevertheless, the sea continued to attract the menfolk of the coastal communities of Ceredigion. The tradition of seafaring was by that time deeply ingrained and despite its manifest hardships, most of the mariners of the area could not contemplate any other way of life. From the 1860s onwards, therefore, an ever-increasing number of sailors from Ceredigion came to take berths on vessels sailing from the major ports of the British Isles to all parts of the world. London, Liverpool and the ports of Tyne, Wear and Tees all became regular embarkation points for sailors from West Wales, though the port that exercised the most powerful hold upon sailors from the area, without doubt, was Cardiff.

An artist's impression of the Bute Docks, Cardiff, in 1894

During the 1860s there was a rapid and spectacular growth in steam-coal mining in the valleys of South Wales and Cardiff was the natural coastal gateway to the mineral wealth of the Taff and its tributaries, such as the Rhondda and the Cynon. Prior to the development of the coal reserves Cardiff's shipping had been relatively insignificant, but during the last quarter of the nineteenth century it became clear that a huge fleet of ships would be needed to distribute coal to the ever-expanding world market. The new prosperity of the port was to be exploited by a generation of immigrant shipowners who came from all over the British Isles. For instance, John Cory, W.J. Tatem and William Reardon Smith were West Countrymen, while the Morels and the Hacquoils were natives of Jersey. From closer to Cardiff came Henry Radcliffe, a native of Merthyr Tudful, who had gained considerable commercial experience with one of Cardiff's earlier shipowners, J.H. Anning, and in June 1881, he and Captain Evan Thomas of Aber-porth launched one of Cardiff's best-known tramp shipping companies, Evan Thomas, Radcliffe and Co.[1]

Evan Thomas of Dol-wen, Aber-porth, came from a background almost identical with that of James and David Jenkins. His father, Hezekiah, owned the coastal trading ketch *Pheasant,* but Evan had forsaken the coastal trade and was an experienced steam tramp master when he decided to venture into ship-owning with Henry Radcliffe in the early 1880s. He himself became master of their first ship, the S.S.*Gwenllian Thomas* of 1882, but as the company prospered in the 'coal out, grain home' trade of the late nineteenth century, further ships were added to their fleet. By 1892 Evan Thomas, Radcliffe managed fifteen vessels, all registered as single ship companies, each one backed by finance raised chiefly in Wales.[2]

As Radcliffe's fleet expanded it was only natural that the company should look to Ceredigion for mariners to man their vessels. Among the masters from Aber-porth whom they recruited during their first decade were James and David Jenkins, who were to become shipowners themselves. Both had gained their master's certificates at Liverpool in 1884,[3] though apart from the fact that they had gone to sea in their fathers' coastal sailing vessels, nothing is known about their seafaring careers prior to their becoming masters. David was the first to join Evan Thomas, Radcliffe, becoming master of the S.S.*Iolo Morgannwg* in 1888 followed by the S.S.*W.I.Radcliffe* during the subsequent year. He remained as master of the latter vessel for nearly seven years and before he left active sea-faring late in 1898 he commanded three other early Radcliffe tramp steamers – the S.S.*Ethel Radcliffe,* S.S.*Llandudno* and S.S.*Clarissa Radcliffe.*

James Jenkins joined Evan Thomas, Radcliffe early in 1890, having previously been master of the S.S.*Iolani* that belonged to the Glasgow company, Raeburn and Vérel. His first command with Radcliffe's was the brand new S.S.*Llanberis* and in 1892 he became master of the S.S.*Mary Thomas.* In 1893, however, James Jenkins left Radcliffe's and became master of the S.S.*Regnant* of Liverpool, owned by R. Conaway and Co. This company owned both sailing and steam vessels and was one of the numerous Liverpool companies that employed a large number of Welsh masters, many from North-West Wales. James Jenkins was not their first master from Ceredigion, however; his cousin Daniel, David's younger brother, had been master of another of

James Jenkins, 1860-1940. Like most Cardiff shipowners of his day, he was always immaculately dressed and invariably wore a flower in his buttonhole

Conaway's vessels, the S.S.*Regimen*, since 1891. Both remained with the company until early in 1896, but at that time James Jenkins retired from active seafaring and turned his attention to the possibility of establishing a ship-owning business in Cardiff in the same way as his former employer had done fifteen years previously.

By July 1896 James Jenkins was established in an office at 129 Bute Street, Cardiff, but it was his father's ketch, *James,* that he was operating from the booming port and not a tramp steamer.[4] This is reflected in the fact that most of the ketch's cargoes in that year were coal outwards from Cardiff, returning with slates from Porthmadog or Caernarfon. A wooden ketch, capable of carrying a mere forty tons of coal, however, was hardly a sound basis for future commercial expansion when the average tramp steamer of the 1890s could carry over a hundred times as much and it seems likely that operating the *James* from Cardiff was only a stop-gap while James Jenkins looked for a suitable steam vessel.

Despite the considerable sum required to purchase a steam cargo vessel, the business of setting up as a shipowner presented relatively few difficulties to persons of initiative and enterprise. To purchase a steam tramp under the old sixty-four share system meant that a small number of quite wealthy investors had to be attracted; shares in Radcliffe's first vessel, which was divided into sixty-fourths, for instance cost £277-7-0d each, a substantial investment at that time. With the advent of joint stock limited liability companies in the mid-

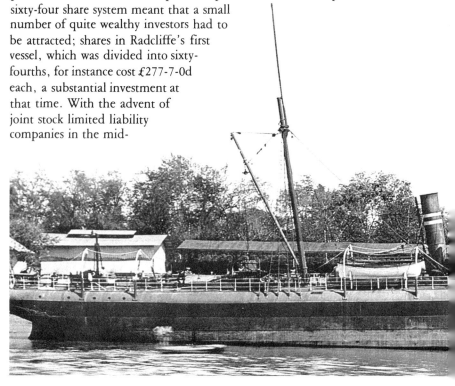

22

nineteenth century, however, it was possible to divide shares into smaller denominations, thus attracting investments from a far wider range of prospective share-holders.[5] From the 1870s onwards, smaller individual entrepreneurs took advantage of limited liability by establishing what came to be known as 'single-ship companies'. This method of ownership imparted numerous advantages; with each company generally owning only one ship, liability for collision damage was limited and the funds of smaller investors could be solicited to set up new companies as further ships were acquired. Ships owned under this system were nominally independent companies, but were in effect linked by the managing owners who had promoted the companies, and who generally controlled numerous vessels. They risked very little of their own money in such ventures; the capital to float the companies was accumulated from a large number of small shareholders, while the managing owners took as their remuneration, not a cut of the profits, but a commission on gross earnings.[6] Thus, as long as the ship was at sea carrying cargo, it did not matter much to the manager whether voyages showed a profit or not. The system was open to some degree of abuse, but it did have the advantage of enabling a relatively rapid growth in the shipping of expanding ports such as Cardiff in the late nineteenth century.

*The S.S.*Gathorne
discharging coal at Seville in 1897

James Jenkins's entry into the world of Cardiff tramp shipping centred around a twenty-four year old iron steamer, the S.S.*Gathorne*. She was an interesting vessel in that she was one of the relatively few steam ships built at Cardiff, at Hill's Dry Docks. These dry docks had been established off the Bute East Dock (then under construction) in 1857 by Messrs. Charles Hill and Sons of Bristol, the noted shipbuilders and founders of the well-known Bristol 'City' Line, and the S.S.*Gathorne* was the last of five vessels that were built at Cardiff by the company between 1862 and 1873.[7] She was sold by her owners, Fisher, Renwick & Co. of Newcastle-upon-Tyne, late in 1896 and in January 1897 the Gathorne Steamship Co. Ltd. was registered at Companies House with James Jenkins as managing owner and a capital of £5,000 divided into 500 shares at £10 each.[8] An Aber-porth master mariner, Captain Simon Thomas (who had been a master on Radcliffe's early tramps at the same time as James and David Jenkins) was given command of the vessel and her first voyage for the company was carrying coal to Seville, returning to Cardiff with iron ore from Bilbao.

Within a relatively short period of time, however, the new company was experiencing financial difficulties. It is clear from the initial shareholders' list that James Jenkins had hoped to attract sufficient capital to float the company in his native village; of the twenty-seven shareholders listed, twenty lived in Aber-porth itself, while a further four lived in nearby towns and villages such as Cardigan or Cwm-cou. Southern Ceredigion in the late nineteenth century could hardly be described, however, as an abundantly wealthy area; despite the fact that there was a well-established coastal trade, it should be borne in mind that it was not very lucrative, existing chiefly to serve a limited agricultural and domestic market. Thus, while there were a few relatively wealthy families in many of the coastal villages of Southern Ceredigion – families like that to which James Jenkins himself belonged who had been involved in the coasting trade and the subsequent retail of the cargoes carried by the locally owned vessels – it could hardly be said that the population of the area, taken as a whole, was particularly fertile ground for the prospective share salesman. Only £2,820 had been raised by the sale of shares in the Gathorne Steamship Co. by the autumn of 1897 and on 7 February 1898 the company was liquidated and the assets transferred to a new concern, the Celtic Shipping Co. Ltd., with James Jenkins and W.J. Williams of 31, Mount Stuart Square, Cardiff, as managing owners.

James Jenkins's new partner was a native of Bethesda who had first found employment in a shipping office in Liverpool. In the late 1880s he moved to Cardiff and took a post at Radcliffe's, where he had risen to become chief cashier before joining James Jenkins early in 1898.[9] The combination of sea-going and commercial experience manifested in the partnership of James Jenkins and W.J. Williams was typical of the teams running many Cardiff shipping ventures at the turn of the century and both partners were obviously

Captain Simon Thomas, 'Glasfor', Aber-porth with the crew of the S.S.Gathorne at Seville in 1897

indebted to Evan Thomas, Radcliffe & Co., in whose service they had become acquainted with the many and varied skills needed to run a shipping company.

The new Celtic Shipping Co. had a capital of £11,700, more than twice the sum raised to finance the Gathorne Steamship Co. It would appear that the remainder of the capital was used to purchase a second iron tramp steamer of similar antiquity to the S.S.*Gathorne*. The S.S.*North Tyne* had been built in 1870 by C. Mitchell and Co. of Newcastle-upon-Tyne and had been the property of four different Tyneside shipowners before her sale to the Celtic Shipping Co. in the late spring of 1898. Thus by mid-1898 the company possessed two tramp steamers, both at least a quarter of a century old, whose iron hulls and compound engines had already been outdated by the rapid developments that took place in shipbuilding during the latter decades of the nineteenth century.[10] Nevertheless, a brand new steel triple expansion-engined tramp would have cost twice as much as both the S.S.*Gathorne* and the S.S.*North Tyne* together and it was probably thought that the purchase of two older vessels was a more effective deployment of the limited capital available.

The Celtic Shipping Co.'s capital of £11,700 was divided into 1,170 shares at £10 each, this being typical of the share denominations available under joint stock limited companies.[11] The new company was almost fully subscribed by July 1898, with a hundred shares held by various members of the Jenkins family in Cardiff and Aber-porth, together with twenty shares held by the family of Miss Catherine Jones of Llanfair P.G., Anglesey, James Jenkins's fiancée. 98% of the capital was raised in Wales, with the shareholders from the Aber-porth area who had invested in the Gathorne Steamship Co. holding roughly the same number of shares in the new company. Their investments, however, constituted only 11% of the capital of the Celtic Shipping Co. and it was clear that under the new directorate, a concerted share sales drive had been mounted in the industrialised areas of Wales. Over a third of the capital was raised among the miners and colliery employees of Glamorgan and Monmouth, while substantial sums also came from the slate quarrying communities of North Wales, particularly from Bethesda and its outlying hamlets where the combined influence of W.J. Williams and the family of James Jenkins's future wife (who were natives of Llanllechid) was probably particularly effective. Of those investors who gave their occupations, almost a half were either colliers or quarrymen (suggesting that despite the arduous and unpleasant nature of their employment, they were by no means poor, being more than willing to invest their savings in shipping ventures in both Liverpool and Cardiff), while a further third were small businessmen and shopkeepers. With the exception of those from the Aber-porth area and one Cardiff chandler, none had any obvious maritime connections; most were small-scale investors with no particular interest in shipping other than that they hoped to make a modest profit from Cardiff's rapidly expanding commercial and shipping enterprises.

CHAPTER 3

Jenkins, Williams & Co., 1898-1904

All the vessels operated by the various Jenkins-managed companies between 1897 and 1927 were tramp steamers. Whereas passenger and cargo liners operated a scheduled service between certain specified ports, a tramp vessel could, theoretically, be chartered to carry any cargo to or from any port at any time, provided that the venture was both legal and safe. Thus the tramp shipping sector of the British shipping industry was dependant upon the prices of a host of different commodities around the world and was always prone to periodic fluctuations in the market.[1] Coal was always available as an outward cargo from various British ports at the turn of the century, but the profitability of voyages depended to a considerable degree upon the securing of a homeward cargo at an advantageous rate.

The entry of James Jenkins and W.J. Williams into tramp shipping coincided with a period when coal exports from the ports of South Wales were steadily increasing and when there were plentiful homeward cargoes of cereals available from the Black Sea. Moreover, the last few years of the 1890s witnessed a welcome respite from the depression that had affected merchant shipping since the early 1870s. It is against this background that the expansion of the partners' enterprise in 1899 and 1900 must be viewed.

The Merchants' Exchange on the Pierhead in Butetown, Cardiff. The company's office was moved to this building in May 1899. (Cardiff Central Reference Library)

In May 1899 the partners moved to an office in the Merchants' Exchange, built earlier on a site now occupied by the Welsh Industrial and Maritime Museum and it was from these premises that they were to continue to expand their shipping interest at the turn of the century. Many shipowners took full advantage of the economic recovery of the time by acquiring second-hand tonnage at quite a rapid rate[2] and before the end of 1900 Jenkins, Williams & Co. had promoted five new single-ship companies, controlling between them over 13,000 gross tons of shipping. None of this tonnage was new, though all of it was considerably more modern than that controlled already by the partners.

The first of these new companies was the Rowtor Steamship Co. Ltd., registered on 22 November 1898 with a capital of £15,000.[3] The S.S.*Rowtor* had been built in 1891 by E. Withy & Co. of West Hartlepool and with her steel hull and triple expansion steam engine, she was a far more up-to-date vessel than either the S.S.*Gathorne* or the S.S.*North Tyne*. She had been built for the well-known London tramp shipping company of J. Holman & Sons and it was this firm that sold her to Jenkins, Williams & Co. late in 1898. Soon afterwards, on 3 January 1899, the Powis Steamship Co. Ltd. was registered with a capital of £12,000 to acquire the S.S.*County*, a steel screw steamer completed by Palmers' of Newcastle-upon-Tyne in November 1889.[4] Purchased new by the Durham Steamship Co. (managed by J. White of Newcastle) and later acquired by McLaren & McLaren of Glasgow, she was re-named S.S.*Powis* after her purchase by the company. She was the only vessel that was re-named by any of the Jenkins-managed companies between 1897 and 1927 and it is probable that the name was taken from Dinas Powis where James Jenkins was living at the time,

The S.S.Rowtor, *acquired in 1898, is seen here in the Avon Gorge approaching Bristol Docks. (World Ship Photo Library)*

28

rather than from the ancient principality of Powys in Mid Wales. She was also the only vessel whose port of registry was changed upon purchase, from Newcastle to Cardiff.

The three remaining companies were floated in 1900. On 12 January the Straits of Menai Steamship Co. Ltd. was registered with a capital of £21,000 to purchase the steel screw steamer S.S.*Straits of Menai*.[5] This vessel had been completed in September 1894 at Furness Withy's West Hartlepool shipyard for N. McLean of Glasgow. Sold again in 1896 to R.B. Stoker of London and later to the British Maritime Trust (a shipowning firm floated by Christopher Furness in 1888[6]) she was acquired by Jenkins, Williams & Co. early in 1900. In November 1900 she was joined by two further tramp steamers, the S.S.*Farringford* and the S.S.*Italiana*. Both were quite recent vessels; the S.S.*Farringford* had been completed by J.L. Thompson & Sons of Sunderland in July 1896 for the Farringford Steamship Co. (Charlton & Thompson of Sunderland, managers) while the S.S.*Italiana* was a mere two years old, having been completed by R. Duncan & Co. of Port Glasgow for the British Maritime Trust in October 1898. The company registered on 5 November 1900 to acquire and operate the S.S.*Farringford* was called the Harrogate Steamship Co. Ltd.;[7] while this may well have been done to distinguish it from the Farringford Steamship Co. still being operated by Charlton & Thompson at Sunderland, there is no accountable reason for the choice of the name Harrogate as a title for the new company. The Italiana Steamship Co. Ltd. was registered later in the month on 26 November.[8]

*The S.S.*Farringford *in ballast trim, with her bows apparently having touched the foreshore off Cardiff, c.1905*

It was generally the practice that single-ship companies were capitalised at, or very near, the purchase price of the vessel. It is clear, however, that the nominal capital of the companies promoted by Jenkins, Williams & Co. in 1899 and 1900 was generally some way below the purchase price of the steamers concerned. The nominal capital of the Powis Steamship Co., for example was £12,000 whereas the vessel cost the company £18,000. Similarly, while the S.S.*Farringford* and the S.S.*Italiana* cost £40,500 and £35,750 respectively, the companies floated to acquire the vessels were capitalised at £35,000 and £26,000 respectively. The balance in each case would appear to have been discharged by a mortgage raised upon the company's vessel, so that by the time that such an amount had been paid off, the overall cost of the vessel would have been reduced.

Shares in the Rowtor and Powis Steamship Companies cost £50 each, five times as much as those of the Celtic Shipping Co. This would seem to have had some effect upon the sources of capital, for the number of investors from the Aber-porth area dropped appreciably, while more shares were purchased by English investors. No-one from James Jenkins's native village invested in the Powis Steamship Co. and only three from Aber-porth bought shares in the S.S.*Rowtor*, while 18% and 11% of the shares in the respective companies were purchased by a wide range of English investors. The vast majority of the capital in both companies, however, still originated among the industrial communities of North and South Wales; about a half of the capital of both companies was provided chiefly by colliers and slate quarrymen. 54% of the capital of the Rowtor Steamship Co. came from the industrial communities of Glamorgan and Monmouth, while the influence of W.J. Williams remained strong in North Wales with some 30% of the capital of the Powis Steamship Co. coming from Caernarfonshire and to a lesser degree, Anglesey. An editorial in the *Maritime Review* early in 1904 acknowledged the debt that many Cardiff shipowners owed to the small investors of North Wales.

'Without the assistance of our kinsmen in North Wales, Lancashire and elsewhere we are prone to admit that the rapid progress made in connection with Cardiff shipowning could not have been made'.[9]

A trend towards increasing investments from England became evident in the shareholders' lists of the companies floated in 1900. All had share denominations of £100 to finance the somewhat more expensive vessels purchased during that year and this would appear to have made the 'Cardis' even more wary of investing in the locally-founded shipping venture, with only three investors from Aber-porth in any of the companies! Just over a quarter of the shares in the Italiana Steamship Co., however, were bought by English investors, the majority of whom were from the North of England with interests in woollen and cotton mills. Indeed, such was the share capital that flowed into Cardiff shipping firms from Lancashire and Yorkshire that the *Maritime Review* asserted that

'. . . some towns 'up North' could be painted red with their faith in the dividend-paying capacity of Cardiff's leviathans'. [10]

The faith of the northern cotton-spinners in Cardiff's shipping was such that five Lancashire entrepreneurs who had emigrated to Russia to set up cotton mills near Moscow bought shares in the Italiana Steamship Co. Furthermore, 22% of the investors in the Harrogate Steamship Co. were resident in England, though there was not the same concentration of northern capital evident in the initial shareholders' list of the latter company. Investments came from a wide range of provincial towns and cities as far apart as Truro, Lincoln and Southport. This was all in marked contrast to the attitude of Cardiff investors who displayed a reluctance to invest in any local shipping venture. Only three Cardiffians held shares in the Italiana Steamship Co. and one of them was the dockland chandler Evan Hughes who already held shares in the Celtic Shipping Co. An even more ironic contrast is provided by the fact that there were three times as many shareholders in the Harrogate Steamship Co. resident in the little town of Montgomery (forty miles from the sea and overwhelmingly agricultural in character) as there were in Cardiff!

It was upon the industrial valleys of South-East Wales that the companies floated in 1900 once again relied for a substantial slice of their capital. Of the 179 investors in the Italiana Steamship Co., over a fifth were miners, while just over a half of the shareholders in the Harrogate Steamship Co. were from the mining valleys of Glamorgan and Monmouth. Shopkeepers and small businessmen were also evident in all three companies, making up about a quarter of the investors who provided descriptions of their occupation in each share list. There was also a scattering of professional men, such as accountants, lawyers, schoolmasters and a number of Nonconformist ministers, mostly of the Calvinistic Methodist denomination to which both James Jenkins and W.J. Williams belonged. The partners themselves and their families held no more than half a dozen shares in each company.

By the beginning of 1901 Jenkins, Williams & Co. were operating no fewer than seven steamships. Unfortunately for the partners, however, the brief boom that had characterised the turn of the century had passed[11] and it was soon deemed prudent to rationalise the fleet by selling off some of the older tonnage. The two old iron steamers with which the partners had inaugurated their venture were the obvious vessels to dispose of and in the spring of 1901 the Celtic Shipping Co. sold the S.S.*Gathorne* to John Raine of Sunderland. Following this sale, a reduction in the capital of the company from £11,700 to £5,850 was approved in the High Court on 4 May[12] and the capital was distributed as a £5 dividend to each shareholder. This sale left the Celtic

Shipping Co. with one vessel, the S.S.*North Tyne*, though she was not sold for some time afterwards.

Despite the onset of depression, the partners' vessels were all fully employed in the early years of the decade. Cargoes of coal outward from Cardiff to the bunkering stations of the Mediterranean were complemented by homeward cargoes of grain from Black Sea ports such as Odessa, Novorossisk and Sulina. These grain cargoes were usually discharged at continental ports such as Antwerp or Hamburg, with the vessels then sailing in ballast back to the Bristol Channel to load coal once more. Between February and December 1903, for instance, the following voyages were undertaken by the S.S.*Rowtor* under the command of Captain Daniel Jenkins, Tre-saith.[13]

Date of sailing	Cargo	From	To
12 February 1903	Coal	Penarth	Malta
2 March 1903	In ballast	Malta	Sulina
19 March 1903	Barley	Sulina	Antwerp
22 April 1903	In ballast	Antwerp	Barry
3 May 1903	Coal	Barry	Genoa
24 May 1903	In ballast	Genoa	Odessa
9 June 1903	Wheat	Odessa	Hamburg
11 July 1903	In ballast	Hamburg	Barry
19 July 1903	Coal	Barry	Marseilles
1 August 1903	In ballast	Marseilles	Odessa
20 August 1903	Wheat	Odessa	Bergen
20 September 1903	In ballast	Bergen	Newport
29 September 1903	Coal	Newport	Genoa
21 October 1903	In ballast	Genoa	Sulina
6 November 1903	Maize	Sulina	Bristol
10 December 1903	In ballast	Bristol	Cardiff

It was often the case that delays were experienced in the Mediterranean and Black Sea ports during the discharging and loading of cargoes. At Sulina, for instance, vessels had to load from lighters and barges that had transported the grain down the Danube and delays caused by the irregular arrival of lighters were common. The S.S.*Rowtor* arrived at Sulina on 9 March 1903 after a stormy passage from Malta and four days later Captain Jenkins noted in his letter book,

'. . . there is no work being done — no lighter down for us, but they are expecting a lighter down for us tomorrow morning'.

It was not until the evening of 14 March that the first lighter arrived and loading was eventually completed on 20 March. Delays were also experienced discharging coal at Genoa in October 1903. The S.S.*Rowtor* reached the Italian port on 4 October and although some of the cargo was taken off by lighter, it was not until 14 October that the vessel was able to obtain a quayside berth where discharging could be effected more rapidly. Even then, however, matters did not proceed smoothly; bad weather and saints' days caused further delays. The last of the cargo was not discharged until 31 October and demurrage was incurred on the last ten days that the S.S.*Rowtor* lay at Genoa. It was not unusual, however, for tramping vessels to spend as many, if not more, days in port than at sea and this was just as true of the busy ports of Northern Europe (where the sheer congestion of the ports often delayed discharging) as it was of Mediterranean and Black Sea ports.

A clear indication of continuing depression in both shipping and ship-building was given in May 1904 when J.L. Thompson of Sunderland, the builder of the S.S.*Farringford,* launched a vessel of the same size for Sunderland owners. Whereas the S.S.*Farringford* had cost £40,500 second-hand in 1900, the second identical vessel was offered for £25,500 off the stocks in 1904 and it was thought that this sum would have to be reduced substantially before a sale could be made.[14] With the industry still at this low ebb, it was decided to dispose of the thirty-four year old S.S.*North Tyne.* She was eventually sold in March 1904 to G.A. Gaponoff of Odessa and re-named after her new owner. Two months later, on 30 May 1904 the Celtic Shipping Company was liquidated by W.J. Williams and the capital distributed among the shareholders. An unspecified sum was also paid as compensation to the managers for loss of management.

*The S.S.*Straits of Menai, *seen here in the house colours of Williams & Mordey, her owners from 1906 until 1910*

Later in 1904 came the first major upheaval in the history of the Jenkins's shipping venture, when W.J. Williams decided to leave the partnership. On 21 September 1904 he wrote to the Register of Joint Stock Companies,

'Sir,

I beg to inform you that the registered office of the Straits of Menai Steamship Company Ltd. has been changed from Merchant's Exchange, Cardiff, to 1, Pierhead Chambers, Cardiff.

Yours faithfully,

W.J. Williams'.[15]

On the 6 and 7 October 1904 he resigned his directorship in all the single-ship companies apart from the Straits of Menai Steamship Co., of which he became sole director and manager. During the following year W.J. Williams operated the S.S.*Straits of Menai* alone, but in January 1906 he went into partnership with T.H. Mordey to form the company of Williams and Mordey; at the time of W.J. Williams's death on 29 June 1913 they managed three steamers from their offices at Boston Buildings in Butetown. [16] While there is no evidence available as to why the partnership was terminated it would appear to have been an amicable arrangement, for both James and David Jenkins and members of their families held shares in the Straits of Menai Steamship Co. until it was finally wound up in January 1912. Thus the Jenkins's connection with North Wales (which had proved to be extremely valuable in the capitalisation of their early single-ship companies) was severed and the loss of this association was to be seen quite evidently in the composition of the shareholders of the later companies promoted by James and David Jenkins.

CHAPTER 4

Daniel Jenkins's Shipping Ventures, 1903-1910

When Jenkins, Williams & Co. vacated their offices at 31, Mount Stuart Square in 1899 little could they have thought that within four years another member of the Jenkins family would have established a shipping company at those premises. He was Daniel Jenkins, David's younger brother (who appears as no.4 in the family tree and should not be confused with his cousin, Captain Daniel Jenkins, who appears as no.6) and he had served previously as master of the S.S.*Regimen* owned by the Liverpool shipping company. R. Conaway & Co.

It is unclear what Daniel Jenkins was doing between the time when he retired from active sea-faring in 1896 until he ventured into shipowning in 1903. Though living in Penarth at the time, he did not invest in any of the companies founded by Jenkins, Williams & Co. around the turn of the century and there is no trace of his having been involved in any other branch of the shipping industry in Cardiff during this period.[1] In 1903, however, Daniel Jenkins floated the Aberporth Steamship Co. Ltd. with a capital of £10,000 divided in to a thousand shares of £10 each, to acquire and operate the former Radcliffe tramp steamer S.S.*W.I.Radcliffe,* which was re-named S.S.*Aberporth* after his native village. This vessel, which actually cost the new company £11,080, had been built by Palmers of Newcastle in 1886 and during the intervening seventeen years Evan Thomas, Radcliffe & Co. had operated her regularly in the Black Sea trade. She was, therefore, by no means a new vessel, having already completed almost two decades of hard work and between 1903 and 1905 her new owners found it necessary to implement repairs costing over £3,000 to keep the vessel sea-worthy.[2]

No records of the Aberporth Steamship Co. have survived, though it would appear that from 29 July 1904 Daniel Jenkins also chartered a Norwegian-owned iron tramp steamer of 1,771 gross tons, the S.S.*Raylton Dixon.* Owned at the time by Valentinsen and Kirsebom of Haugesund, she was operated in the Black Sea trade by Daniel Jenkins over a six month period. With the completion of that agreement he subsequently chartered the Lubeck-owned tramp steamer, S.S.*Horta* (1,722 gross tons) for a year until January 1906.[3] In the meantime the S.S.*Aberporth,* too, was chiefly employed on the Black Sea trade and from March 1905 onwards her master was Simon Thomas of Aberporth, who had previously been master of the S.S.*Gathorne.* On 29 April the old steamer sailed from Barry with a cargo of coal for Constantinople. Adverse weather conditions were experienced in the Bay of Biscay and the bilge pumps broke down, causing considerable flooding. These defects were rectified at

The S.S. Aberporth, *built in 1886 as the S.S.* W.I.Radcliffe, *was lost in the Black Sea in June 1905*

Constantinople and the S.S.*Aberporth* then proceeded, not to one of the usual grain ports, but to Poti in the south-eastern extremity of the Black Sea to load 2,500 tons of manganese ore.

On 15 June the S.S.*Aberporth* left Poti and having taken on bunkers at Zoungouldak, sailed for Antwerp on the afternoon of 18 June. At 1.40am the following morning the vessel was some sixteen miles north of Kilia lighthouse, making about eight knots on a smooth sea that was crossed by a heavy grounds-well when the 3rd engineer noted that the bilges were flooding again. He aroused the first engineer, who ordered both bilge and ballast pumps to be started. At 2.00am, Captain Thomas was woken, by which time the steamer was listing to port and shipping far more water than the pumps could handle. Orders were given for the ship to be stopped and the boats lowered; below, the situation was becoming increasingly hopeless as the firemen were waist-deep in water and the engine room was also seriously flooded. With the S.S.*Aberporth* settling on her beam ends, the Captain ordered 'abandon ship' at 3.00am and the boats remained alongside until she finally sank at 5.45am, taking with her to the bottom of the Black Sea the savings of many small investors from Aberporth.[4]

Captain Thomas and the crew of the S.S.*Aberporth*, (that included one of the master's sons, David, a teenager on his first deep-sea voyage) got back to Cardiff in July and a Board of Trade Inquiry was held there from 25 to

30 August 1905. Having ascertained the chronology of events leading up to and including the loss of the vessel, the inquiry then directed attention to particular aspects of the whole episode. It was clear from the rapidity with which the stokehold and engine room had flooded that there had been a sudden and substantial onrush of water, which in the opinion of the inquiry could have been caused only by the bottom of the steamer parting. Here, attention was drawn to the way in which the cargo of ore had been stowed; it had not been distributed evenly in the steamer's four holds, but, with the exception of fifty tons in the aftermost hold, had been divided entirely between the second and third holds, thus creating a tremendous strain amidships. The inquiry was of the opinion that Captain Thomas's mode of stowage was chiefly to blame for the shearing of the vessel's hull, which in turn eventually led to her loss.[5]

Captain Thomas was praised for his promptness in ensuring the safety of the crew, but the inquiry, nevertheless, felt that in his actions he had perhaps abandoned the vessel too soon. It was suggested, for example, that the firemen should have been ordered to remain in the stokehold so that the steam pressure needed to drive the pumps could be maintained. However, as the *Maritime Review* pointed out in an editorial article on the inquiry

'. . . the water was already waist-high (in the stokehold) and lapping the bottom edges of the furnaces . . .'[6]

To have ordered the firemen to remain there any longer would have been tantamount to condemning them to a horrible death in a scalding inferno. It was also suggested that some attempt should have been made to beach the S.S.*Aberporth,* though Captain Thomas stated that with the vessel unable to steam and settling on her beam ends, this was hardly a practical proposition,[7] especially as the coastline ten miles away consisted almost entirely of sheer cliffs rising from the sea. The *Maritime Review* further added

'. . . if S.S.*Aberporth* had been successfully beached, is it to be contended that any sane underwriter would have done any other than have marked her off as a constructive total loss'?[8]

Further questions were raised regarding the insurance of the S.S.*Aberporth.* In summing the case up

'. . . the Court *notes,* but does not feel warranted to make any inferences, that the vessel foundered in fine weather, ten miles from land owing to an obscure cause upon which the officers can throw no light; that the master made no effort to save her and that she was insured at least £5,000 in excess of her true value.'[9]

The inquiry estimated that the vessel was worth at the most £9,000, while the insurance amounted to a total of £16,200 for hull, machinery and freight; if not actually inferring the fact, it was hinted quite strongly that the vessel had been scuttled for insurance purposes. Daniel Jenkins made no statement at the inquiry, but he furnished the *Maritime Review* with correspondence relating to the insurance of the S.S.*Aberporth* on her last voyage. The vessel's considerable age had not made her a particularly attractive proposition to the underwriters and the correspondence published in the *Maritime Review*[10] shows that while Daniel Jenkins had hoped to insure the vessel on the basis of a £13,000 valuation of hull and machinery, he was forced to accept a quotation based upon a £14,000 valuation – a sum which was, moreover, £1,000 less than the lowest valuation he was offered initially. Furthermore, information obtained from Radcliffe's, her previous owners, showed that she had been insured for a total of £20,700 during her last year of service as the S.S.*W.I.Radcliffe*. The vessel was clearly insured in excess of her actual market value at the time of her loss, but this would seem to have been due chiefly to the attitude of the underwriters to the vessel's age rather than a desire on the part of the owner to 'lose' her. The final verdict of the inquiry was that the S.S.*Aberporth*

'. . . sprang a leak and was abandoned. The court finds that the cause cannot be confidently stated.'

Nevertheless, it was thought that the negligent manner in which the cargo had been stowed was a crucial factor in the loss of the vessel and Captain Thomas's certificate was suspended for two years.[11]

The loss of the S.S.*Aberporth* did not signal the demise of Daniel Jenkins as a shipowner, however. He was still chartering the S.S.*Horta* and during 1905 he had embarked upon a rapid and ambitious – albeit ultimately unsuccessful – expansion of his shipping interests. Early in that year, he acquired an interest in two single-ship companies, the Saint Regulus Steamship Co. Ltd. and the Kingsland Steamship Co. Ltd., which had been managed previously by the partnership Eeles, Ruston and McMullen of Cardiff. On 26 May he became the managing owner of both companies in partnership with S.R. Ruston, one of the former managers and moved his offices to 43, The Exchange at about that time. The Saint Regulus Steamship Co. dated from 1902[12] and had been set up to acquire and operate the S.S.*Saint Regulus,* a steam tramp of 3,131 gross tons built in 1886 by T. Royden & Sons of Liverpool for the British and Foreign Steamship Co., Liverpool, (Rankin, Gilmour & Co., managers). The Kingsland Steamship Co. did not possess a ship at the time when Daniel Jenkins and S.R. Ruston took over, having lost its only vessel, the S.S.*Algoma* in July 1904, but in September 1905 a brand new tramp steamer of 2,831 gross tons named S.S.*Kingsland* was completed for the company by the Sunderland Ship-building Co., Sunderland at a cost of £29,000. The company had a nominal capital of £18,000 divided into 1,800 shares at £10 each, the remainder of the cost of the vessel being secured by various unspecified loans and a mortgage from the builders.[13]

By the late summer of 1905, Daniel Jenkins was in the process of setting up a further shipping venture quite separate from that outlined hitherto. On

The S.S. Saint Regulus, *seen here moored in the Thames off Gravesend, was taken over by Daniel Jenkins and S.R. Ruston in 1905. (The National Maritime Museum, London)*

8 September the *Maritime Review* reported that Daniel Jenkins & Co. had ordered a new tramp steamer from Bartram & Sons of Sunderland[14] and on 18 October the well-known shipping magazine *Syren & Shipping* advertised the prospectus of the Tylorstown Steamship Co. Ltd. for whom the steamer was being built at a cost of £35,250. The company had a nominal capital of £25,000 divided into 250 shares at £100 each and had as its managing owners Daniel Jenkins and his second new partner, F.H. Kirkhouse, the son of the well-known mining engineer and coal-owner, Herbert Kirkhouse of Tylorstown.[15] Among the first subscribers to the new company was Sir W.T. Lewis, later Lord Merthyr of Senghenydd, manager of Cardiff's Bute Docks and owner of the Lewis Merthyr Consolidated Collieries. Soon afterwards the partners ordered a further new steamer from the yards of Craig, Taylor & Co. of Stockton-upon-Tees and from November 1905 onwards advertisements for the company of 'Dan Jenkins, Kirkhouse & Co.' appeared regularly in the *Maritime Review*.

With all sectors of the British shipping industry undergoing a period of depression during the first decade of the twentieth century, there existed a buyers' market for new tonnage and it was common practice for owners to buy tonnage when prices were low, in anticipation of a forthcoming improvement in the market. This was probably the thinking that lay behind the new partners' promotion of two new single-ship companies at that time, but within a few months it would appear that their foresight had been ill-conceived. Whereas larger, old-established firms might be able to afford the capital outlay to purchase a new vessel in times of depression, it was an entirely different matter for a small new company to try and attract investment in shipping in such straitened economic circumstances. By the beginning of January 1906 Daniel Jenkins and Frank Kirkhouse had been forced to sell both vessels off the stocks to unspecified owners, probably as a result of their failure to raise sufficient capital to float either company.[16] At the same time Jenkins and Kirkhouse concluded their short-lived partnership and later, in March 1907, Frank Kirkhouse went into shipowning on his own account as managing owner of the Rhondda Steamship Co. Ltd., operating the S.S.*Enterprize* and later the S.S.*Royal Exchange.*

Following this abortive venture Daniel Jenkins turned to concentrate exclusively upon the operation of the S.S.*Saint Regulus* and S.S.*Kingsland.* As a result of the death of S.R. Ruston he became the sole managing owner of the two vessels from 16 May 1906 and despite the continuing adverse economic circumstances, Daniel Jenkins endeavoured to keep both vessels fully employed. In August 1906 he could have lost the S.S.*Saint Regulus* after she had arrived in Valparaiso, Chile, with a cargo of coal from Cardiff. On 17 August the busy port was almost totally devastated by one of the worst earthquakes ever recorded on the South American continent and the tremendous seismographic disturbance reached 8.6 on the Richter scale, worse even than the San Francisco earthquake that had occurred only four months before. In his fascinating book, *Growing Up Among Sailors,* Ifor Davies recalls how his mother, the wife of the master of the well-known barque, *Gwydyr Castle,* watched the steamers at Valparaiso making for the open sea to avoid the tidal waves that followed; the S.S.*Saint Regulus* made her way northwards to the small town of Los Villos to discharge her cargo early in September.[17] Delayed off the coast of Chile well into 1907, it would appear, furthermore, that she was becoming something of a financial liability by that time. From May 1906 onwards, for instance, the Saint Regulus Steamship Co. was forced to take out a number of loans, including one of £3,500 later that year from the Kingsland Steamship Co., in order to continue in operation. Eventually, however, the age of the steamer and the prevailing depression in freight rates led to her being sold at Antwerp in December 1907 to a company of Blyth shipbreakers.

The details of Daniel Jenkins's last years as a shipowner are far from clear, but it would appear that he found himself embroiled in increasing financial problems from 1907 onwards. The S.S.*Kingsland* was trading at a considerable loss; one voyage late in 1907 showed a profit of a mere £77-1-9d and the general profit and loss account for the period July 1907 until October 1908 showed an overall loss in excess of £3,700. After 1908 the subscription registers of the Cardiff & Bristol Channel Incorporated Shipowners' Association show that he was unable to pay his membership fee and his name was struck off the list of members from 1909 onwards.[18] Furthermore, from 1907 onwards he managed the Kingsland Steamship Co., not as Daniel Jenkins & Co., but under the name

The S.S. Kingsland *was completed by the Sunderland Shipbuilding Co. Ltd. in September 1905*

of his deceased partner, S.R. Ruston & Co. He also opened an office at Bristol in 1908, though there is no trace of his having owned any other vessels on the other side of the Bristol Channel.

On 12 March 1909, in an attempt to stave off what would appear to have become an increasingly difficult financial situation, Daniel Jenkins took out a second mortgage on the S.S.*Kingsland* from Herbert Davies-Evans, a Llandeilo banker. It was to prove his undoing, for in March 1910 both Davies-Evans and the Sunderland Shipbuilding Co. foreclosed. Soon afterwards, in response to a demand by the Registrar of Joint Stock Companies to supply Companies' House with the annual returns of the Kingsland Steamship Co., Daniel Jenkins revealed the true extent of his difficulties.

> '. . . the reason why this has not been done is that the mortgagees have taken possession of the steamer owned by the company . . . we would mention, however, that we have a law suit pending with the mortgagees which will determine their right to take possession of the vessel. . .'19

This law suit achieved nothing, for two months later on 23 May 1910, at an Extraordinary General Meeting of the Kingsland Steamship Co. held at Cardiff, it was decided that the company could not, by reason of its liabilities, continue to trade. A liquidator was appointed to deal with the termination of both companies' activities, though it was not until July 1912 that the process was completed and both concerns wound up. From 1910 until 1912 the S.S.*Kings-*

land was managed by Philipps, Philipps & Co. (managers of the King Line) before being sold in 1912 to the Scottish Steamship Co., a subsidiary of the King Line and re-named S.S.*King Arthur*.

Daniel Jenkins's venture into shipowning did not last a decade, and his attempt to emulate the example of his brother and his cousin quite clearly failed. Though not lacking in drive and ambition, he entered into tramp shipping at a time when the market was severely depressed and this was reflected both in the failure to float the two new steamship companies in 1905 and the losses incurred by the S.S.*Saint Regulus* and the S.S.*Kingsland* in later years. Had he been able to last out a little longer, Daniel Jenkins might have been able to reap the advantage of the gradual improvement in freight rates from 1912 onwards, leading to the boom years of the First World War, but this was not to be. Following the bankruptcy of the Kingsland Steamship Co. in 1910 he never again ventured into shipowning, one of the many less successful participants in Cardiff's golden era as a port, whose tale is rarely told.

CHAPTER 5

Jenkins Bros., 1904-1914

Following the departure of W.J. Williams from the partnership of Jenkins, Williams & Co. in October 1904, the managing company, now consisting of the remaining partners James Jenkins and his cousin David Jenkins, was re-named Jenkins Bros. The company's new name stemmed from the fact that the cousins were also brothers-in-law, since David had married his cousin Jane, James's eldest sister. It would appear that David Jenkins (who should not be confused with Captain David Jenkins, 'Pen-parc', Aber-porth, eleventh master listed in the appendix of ships' masters) had not been involved in the foundation of the venture in 1897-98, for he was at sea as master of the S.S. *Clarissa Radcliffe* until late in 1898 and could not have joined the partnership until 1899 when he retired from active sea-faring and took up residence at 66 Penylan Road, Cardiff. As such James Jenkins (who had moved to live in Penarth in 1900) was the 'senior' partner and it was he who took the leading role in the management of the firm from 1904 onwards. One of the first changes that became apparent under the new régime was the adoption of a uniform colour scheme, the ships having black hulls with red 'boot-topping' white superstructures and plain black funnels. A house flag was devised, consisting of a white diamond bearing the letters 'JB' on a red background, while cap badges with this motif are also apparent in crew photographs from *c.* 1908 onwards.

David Jenkins 1860-1919

There was a general upward trend in coal exports from the ports of South Wales during the years preceding the First World War. Cardiff and Barry both exported some 7½ million tons each in 1900, whereas by 1913 the respective figures were 10½ million tons and 11 million tons. Jenkins Bros. continued to rely heavily upon the lucrative Black Sea trade, though from 1905 onwards, the S.S.*Farringford* and the S.S.*Italiana* undertook the occasional voyage to South America, chiefly to Buenos Aires. South America accounted for no more than 15% of Britain's total coal exports before 1914,[1] but the fact that this percentage consisted almost entirely of South Wales steam coal made it an exceptionally significant trade for Cardiff shipowners. The outward cargoes of coal were complemented by homeward cargoes of cereals from River Plate ports such as Rosario. Despite this apparently buoyant picture, however, it was not a particularly favourable period for many tramp shipowners due to the prolonged depression in freight rates that lasted until 1912. During the depths of this depression in 1907 and 1908, freight rates were less than half those prevailing in 1900, affecting both outward and homeward cargoes.[2]

Economic circumstances such as these had a particularly hard effect upon smaller tramp shipping companies operating older vessels. If tramp shipping owners such as those at Cardiff wished their ships to be competitive, their policy had to be determined by balancing wage costs against repair costs. The wage costs of British crews were higher than those of other countries operating substantial tramp fleets (such as Norway or Greece) and it was advantageous, therefore, for British owners to operate newer and larger vessels whose repair bills were low and whose greater deadweight capacity enabled considerable economies of scale to be achieved. Such new vessels, if carefully managed, could be run at a profit even when the freight rates were depressed. British owners operating older vessels, however, were at a disadvantage, for while their wage bills remained much the same, the low speed of their vessels, coupled with repair bills that increased with their age, rapidly transformed what should have been their chief assets into considerable liabilities.[3] It was very difficult, indeed, to make older vessels pay when freight rates were low and this was reflected in the accounts of the seventeen year-old S.S.*Powis* for 1905-06. Her losses in 1905 had forced Jenkins Bros. to make a loan of £1,700 to the Powis Steamship Co. and whereas her five voyages during 1906 accumulated a gross profit in excess of £1,200, when this figure was set against the cost of repairs and renewals in the general profit and loss account, the S.S.*Powis* made an overall loss of £277-2-10d between February and December that year.[4] Such were the problems faced by smaller shipowners operating older vessels when the market was depressed.

During the eighteen months between January 1906 and June 1907, Jenkins Bros. lost two of their older vessels. The first of these losses, that of S.S.*Rowtor* commanded by Captain John Davies of Aber-porth, occurred at 8.40pm on

The S.S. Italiana *entering Antwerp with a cargo of wheat from the Black Sea in July 1905*

3 January 1906 while the fifteen year-old steamer was outward bound from Barry to Port Said with a cargo of coal. After sunset, with visibility further obscured by heavy rain, the vessel struck a reef north of the Fratelli Rocks off the northern coast of Tunisia; despite coming off the reef soon after the impact she sank within an hour, without loss of life.[5] A Board of Trade Inquiry was held at Cardiff on 13 and 14 February 1906, at which much attention was centred upon the course of the vessel at the time of her loss, a course that had been set at 3.30am on 3 January. The S.S.*Rowtor* carried a full set of charts for that part of the Mediterranean and her compass had been overhauled five months previously. It was proved to the satisfaction of the inquiry, therefore, that there had been no navigational error and that the course set by Captain Davies on the day of the loss should have taken the vessel clear of the reef. The inquiry was also of the opinion, however, that Captain Davies had not made allowances for tides and currents and that he was steaming far too quickly in poor visibility without using the lead. The final verdict of the inquiry was that

> 'The immediate cause of the loss was excessive speed and neglect of the lead, caused by the wrongful default of the master'.

and Captain Davies's certificate was suspended for three months.[6]

The loss of the S.S.*Rowtor* left the Rowtor Steamship Co. without a ship and a replacement vessel was ordered almost immediately. With the prevailing depression in shipping the price for new tonnage was low and the partners decided to order their first brand-new vessel from Craig, Taylor and Co. of

45

Stockton-on-Tees. Delivered in October 1906, the S.S.*Glamorgan* was a steel screw steamer of 3,539 gross tons; she cost the Rowtor Steamship Co. £38,890, which worked out at the relatively low price of some £6-10-0d per deadweight ton. Her purchase was financed by a mortgage, not from the builders nor a bank, but from John Holman & Son, the London shipowners who were financing the purchase of a number of vessels by Cardiff owners at that time.[7]

*The S.S.*Glamorgan *was completed by Craig, Taylor & Co. of Stockton-on-Tees in October 1906*

With the price of new tonnage remaining quite low and in hopeful anticipation of future improvements in freight rates, James and David Jenkins ordered a further new steamer in October 1906, this time from the well-known shipowners and builders, Robert Ropner & Sons of Stockton-on-Tees. The S.S. *Cardigan*, as she was later named, was a steel screw steamer of 4,295 gross tons and she was built to Ropner's Patent trunk deck design, originated by the company in 1896. Trunk-decked vessels conferred a number of advantages, among which were a superior deadweight capacity in relation to nett tonnage, increased longitudinal strength and large unobstructed hatches that facilitated rapid loading and discharging.[8] The trunk deck arrangement also afforded considerable savings on trimming charges when loading coal at South Wales ports. The cost of the vessel was £39,930, which at £5-12-6d per deadweight ton, was even cheaper than the S.S. *Glamorgan;* James and David Jenkins emphasised that they had managed to secure

'. . . one of the cheapest vessels ever built . . . since then building material has advanced considerably . . . every keen investor knows that the best time to buy is when building material is low . . .'[9]

A new single-ship company, the Cardigan Steamship Co. Ltd. was registered at Companies' House on 3 April 1907, with a capital of £35,000 divided into 350 shares. The prospectus of the new company (issued in April 1907 and reproduced in the appendices) is interesting in that it reveals the means whereby the single ship company was established and also the relationship between it and the managing firm of Jenkins Bros. The initial contract of October 1906 for the building of the vessel was between Jenkins Bros. and the shipbuilders; then, by an agreement of March 1907, James and David Jenkins undertook to sell the vessel to the Cardigan Steamship Co. at no profit, but on the understanding that they became managing directors of the new company. Their remuneration as managers was 2 ½ % of the gross earnings of the vessel, or 5 % on chartered freight if the vessel was on time charter. Among the initial subscribers to the new company were Sir Walter Runciman the eminent shipowner (for whose company Jenkins Bros. were chartering agents at Cardiff and Barry) and Sir E.J. Webley-Parry-Pryse of Gogerddan near Aberystwyth, who perhaps saw investment in shipping as a means of helping to clear the crippling debts that both he and his estates had incurred at that time.[10]

While shares in the new vessel (due to be delivered in July 1907), were being offered for sale, Jenkins Bros. suffered their second shipping loss under circumstances that were to arouse much comment, both in Cardiff shipping circles and further afield. The S.S. *Powis* sailed from Cardiff on 25 May 1907 under the command of Captain John Phillips, with a cargo of coal bound for Leghorn (Livorno) in Italy. Having discharged this cargo, Captain Phillips then received orders to proceed to Seriphos Island in the Aegean Sea to take on a cargo of iron ore for Middlesborough. On the morning of 20 June the S.S. *Powis* completed loading and she departed at 1.00pm that day; the weather was fine and the wind blowing lightly from the north-west. She proceeded south-west at full speed for some three hours and most of the hands were on deck hosing the iron ore dust off the vessel when Captain Phillips noticed from the bridge that the water on the deck was flowing forwards, rather than aft as the trim of the vessel should have dictated. He ordered the first mate to the fo'c's'le head and was subsequently informed that the vessel was at least five feet down by the head. Shortly after 4.00pm the master stopped the ship and called out '. . . all hands on deck, the ship is sinking . . .' The engineers, who had noted nothing amiss during the three-hour voyage, came on deck to see the boats being provisioned and lowered; Captain Phillips then ordered the first engineer below again to start the pumps. While carrying out this order the first engineer noted no unusual water below, but, nevertheless, having gathered a few personal belongings, he joined the rest of the crew as they abandoned the vessel. With her pumps still going the S.S. *Powis* took over an hour and a half to sink, whereupon the crew, all of whom were saved, set sail for Seriphos. They arrived there at 6.00am the following morning.[11]

*The S.S.*Powis *loading iron ore at Seriphos Island in the Aegean Sea shortly before she foundered and sank on 20 June 1907. (Glamorgan Archive Service)*

A Board of Trade Inquiry was held at the City Law Courts, Cardiff, between 8 and 23 August 1907. It soon became clear that whereas the inquiry had at its disposal an enormous amount of *circumstantial* evidence, little assistance as to the cause of the vessel's loss was afforded by such *direct* evidence as came to light. Indeed, some of the evidence was quite contradictory and nowhere was this more apparent than in the varying accounts of the steamer's three-hour voyage from Seriphos given by the deck officers and the engineers. If the vessel had been five feet down by the head at 4.00pm that day, this would have been evident in the gauge glasses that showed the water level in the boilers, but no such movement was noticed and neither was there evidence of excessive water anywhere below. Moreover, the inquiry was of the opinion that if the vessel had been that far down in the water when she was abandoned, it was highly unlikely that she would have floated so long afterwards. Grave doubts were cast, therefore, on the master's interpretation of events on board the S.S.*Powis* before 4.00pm; the inquiry thought it most unlikely that she could have lost her freeboard so suddenly without anyone having noticed, especially as most of the crew was on deck clearing the ore dust off the vessel.

Captain Phillips was also criticised severely for his action in abandoning the vessel so quickly. Though he ordered the first engineer to return to the engineroom to start up all the pumps, he made no attempt to ascertain the whereabouts of the leak, neither did he wait to see whether the starting of the pumps had any beneficial effect and this despite the fact that the ship remained afloat for an hour and a half afterwards. Instead, he concentrated entirely upon provisioning the lifeboats and getting them over the side, making no effort whatsoever to inspire confidence and maintain discipline. The entire crew thus became

'. . . infected by the general fear evidently generated by the alleged phenomenon . . . the evidence clearly establishes that the vessel was prematurely abandoned and was not navigated with proper and seamanlike care.'[12]

In his defence Captain Phillips stated that they had been loading for four days at Seriphos, where the ore was tipped through a chute into the holds of the vessel, falling some forty feet when the vessel was unladen. Much of the ore was in large lumps weighing at least five hundredweight, which struck the bottom of the hold with a force that caused the entire vessel to shudder. On 10 August Captain Phillips told the inquiry that he attributed

'. . . the incoming of water to the fracturing of the plates by the heavy masses of ore shot into the hold . . .',[13]

while W.B. Jenkins of Solfach, bosun of the S.S.*Powis,* also confirmed that the vessel had been subjected to repeated heavy blows while loading the ore. William Pepperell, the first mate, maintained, however, that he had checked the cargo in the holds after loading had been completed and was satisfied that no structural damage had been suffered by the ship. The inquiry concurred with the latter opinion and then turned to consider a far more serious question, namely,

'. . . whether the cause of the water was wilfully put into operation by human agency . . .'[14]

The inquiry acknowledged that it was very difficult to produce any direct evidence to prove or disprove this assumption, especially as it had been impossible to find any evidence of any preparations by the master or the crew to scuttle the vessel. The act, if at all capable of proof, could be proved only by inference and presumption. Nevertheless, the question was posed whether either the master or the managing owner had any motive for scuttling the vessel and after subjecting the witnesses to much brow-beating the inquiry revealed some unusual financial arrangements between Captain Phillips and the crew of the S.S.*Powis,* on one hand, and James Jenkins on the other, both before and after the loss of the vessel. When the crew was paid off on 2 July, having returned to Cardiff, Captain Phillips had retained £29, being the difference between the total wage bill and the sum he had received to pay off the crew. This was said to be in part repayment of a loan of £300 made by Captain Phillips to the Powis Steamship Co. in 1905, the consideration being that he should be appointed master of the S.S.*Powis.* Moreover, in addition to their wages, the sum of £112 was distributed among the rest of the crew before making their statements to the Receiver of Wreck and on condition that they signed a document declaring that they were receiving the money '. . . purely as an act of charity'. Thus the master had a clear financial interest in the Powis Steamship Co., as (in an indirect manner) had the crew members who had received the gratuity from the company.[15]

The significance of the master's financial interest in the Powis Steamship Co. was highlighted when the inquiry moved on to consider the insurance of the S.S.*Powis.* She was reckoned by her owners to be worth £12,000 at the time of her loss, though a figure as low as £9,500 was postulated by Mr. Blackitt, a marine engineer appearing on behalf of the shippers of the cargo. She was, nevertheless, insured for a total of £24,125 when she departed from Seriphos, this sum comprising £16,000 for hull and machinery, £1,500 for freight and a total of £6,625 for premiums and disbursements. Hence the insurances as a whole exceeded the value of the vessel by some £9,000. As in the case of the S.S.*Aberporth,* the age of the S.S.*Powis* meant that she could be insured only at enhanced premiums, though while this partly explained the excessive insurance, the report of the inquiry was also explicit in the way that it drew attention to aspects of the Powis Steamship Co.'s trading record in relation to the insurance policies;

'. . . the vessel was trading at a loss, she was nineteen years old, she had her original boilers . . . she was deeply in debt and was insured for £5,000 in excess of her value . . .

summarizing the evidence on the question of foul play; the master had *some,* the managing owner a *strong* motive for throwing the vessel away.' [16]

The inference was only too clear and it was even proposed in the concluding paragraphs of the inquiry report that the entire affair should be brought to the attention of the Public Prosecutor. Inferences do not, however, constitute evidence and despite the fact that one of the conclusions of the inquiry was that

'. . the probable cause was put into operation by human agency . . .',

no firm evidence either to prove or disprove this assumption could be produced. By late September the Public Prosecutor had decided that there was insufficient evidence to proceed with the case. Nevertheless, it was within the powers of the inquiry to discipline Captain Phillips; he was found guilty of gross negligence conducive to the loss of the vessel and lost his ticket for eighteen months. [17]

The inquiry was the subject of considerable comment, both during its duration and afterwards. Detailed reports of each day's proceedings appeared in the *Western Mail* and the *South Wales Daily News.* London shipping journals such as *Syren and Shipping* and *Fairplay* were deeply critical of the entire affair, particularly with regard to the question of over-insurance, though the Cardiff-based *Maritime Review* was stout in its defence of both master and managing owner, believing them to have been

'. . . the butt of a smug number of legally-trained intellects.' [18]

What exactly happened in the Aegean Sea on a June afternoon in 1907 will (as the inquiry was eventually forced to admit) probably never be known. Once the Public Prosecutor had decided not to pursue the case, the insurance claims were settled later that year. The proceeds were not used, however, to buy a new vessel for the Powis Steamship Co.; most of the sum was invested by the purchase of shares in the Cardigan Steamship Co., a vital injection of capital that was not only crucial in floating the latter company, but which also made the Powis Steamship Co. the largest single shareholder in the S.S.*Cardigan.*

The S.S.*Cardigan* had been delivered on 12 July 1907; her purchase price was secured by a mortgage of £28,700 with interest at 5%, from Ropner's, her builders. Just over a half of the investors in the new vessel came, once again, from Glamorgan and Monmouth, though in marked contrast to the composition of shareholders in the previous single-ship companies, there was only one shareholder from North Wales in the Cardigan Steamship Co. This may well have been a result of the departure of W.J. Williams from the firm over two years previously; his association with the slate-quarrying districts of Caernarfonshire had formerly brought substantial injections of capital from the quarrymen and small businessmen of communities such as Bethesda. If investment was no longer forthcoming in North Wales, however, James and David Jenkins would appear to have conducted a successful sales campaign in

*The first S.S.*Cardigan, *completed by Ropner's of Stockton-on-Tees in July 1907, was built to the trunk deck design first introduced by the builders in 1896*

their native village and its immediate vicinity; nine persons from the Aberporth area invested in the S.S.*Cardigan,* including three master mariners and an engineer employed by the company. Among other investors in the new steamer were steamship agents from Leghorn (Livorno) and Sulina, who were probably hopeful of gaining the agency for the S.S.*Cardigan* when she traded to those ports.

By the end of 1907, therefore, Jenkins Bros. were operating four tramp steamers, two dating from the late 1890s and two which were relatively new. The prevailing depression in freight rates, however, was still having a serious effect upon shipping throughout the world, especially on tramp shipping and the firm was not left unscathed by these unfavourable economic circumstances. The S.S.*Italiana* was laid up at Barry for three months from 10 June 1908, while the two newer vessels showed no profit from their trading in 1908 nor 1909. The effects of the depression were quite marked in the falling-off of homeward freight rates from the Black Sea in the years prior to the outbreak of the First World War. Fewer voyages were made to the Black Sea by the firm's vessels during the six years before 1914; this was particularly true of the S.S.*Glamorgan* and the S.S.*Cardigan,* both of which undertook tramping voyages in the Indian and Pacific Oceans at that time, returning to Europe with cargoes of cereals from Australia. There were also occasional voyages to the eastern seaboard of the U.S.A. The prevailing economic circumstances were reflected in despondent and gloomy articles in shipping journals; in September 1908, the Cardiff-based *Maritime Review* concluded an editorial article with these lines

'. . . meanwhile, the depression continues and those with most knowledge of the subject are most averse to give an opinion as to what the end is likely to be. Certainly the silver lining is anything but in sight at the moment.'[19]

The clouds at last began to assume a silver lining for the shipowners in 1912 when freight rates once more began to return to the levels at which they had stood at the turn of the century. This was reflected in the balance sheets of the four single-ship companies, which by the end of 1912 all showed a profit, albeit a small one that cannot have paid much of a dividend to shareholders. By 1913, there was a further improvement in profits; the Harrogate Steamship Co. that operated the S.S.*Farringford,* for instance, showed a profit of a mere £44-18-7d in a balance sheet of June 1912, but by July 1913 the profit was over a hundred times greater at £4,850-3-5d.[20] With the improvement in freight rates, Jenkins Bros. decided that it would be wise to invest in a further vessel before building prices rose substantially in the more buoyant market prevailing at the time; accordingly, in December 1913, they placed an order with Richardson, Duck & Co. of Stockton-on-Tees for a tramp steamer of some 4,500 gross tons. Delivered on 7 July 1914 the S.S.*Anglesea,* as she was named, was a shelter-decked steel screw steamer of a little over 7,000 deadweight tons; at £55,329, she cost some £7-18-0d per deadweight ton, showing the increase in building prices that had occurred since the completion of the S.S.*Cardigan* in 1907. Her purchase was financed by a mortgage for an unspecified sum from the London City and Midland Bank, though no new single-ship company was floated to raise capital for the new ship. Instead, the S.S.*Anglesea* became part of the property of the Cardigan Steamship Co., though it was not until July 1915 that the company's capital was increased to take account of the acquisition of the new steamer.

The two years immediately prior to the outbreak of the First World War constituted the high noon of Cardiff's coal trade. In 1913, a staggering total of 26 million tons of coal was exported from Cardiff, Penarth and Barry. Less than a month after the delivery of the S.S.*Anglesea* in July 1914, however, Britain declared war on Germany after the invasion of Belgium. Not only did this war transform the character of early twentieth century Europe, but it also had far-reaching consequences that profoundly affected the coal and shipping industries of South Wales.

CHAPTER 6

Masters and Mariners

During the latter half of the nineteenth century, maritime activity in the coastal towns and villages of Southern Ceredigion was all-embracing, claiming to a considerable degree most of the time of the inhabitants of those communities. The routines of daily and seasonal work in villages such as Aber-porth or Llangrannog revolved more around the sea and its associated activities, than around agriculture. In the spring the local trading smacks and ketches would put to sea again, having been laid up on the River Teifi over the winter and would soon be seen arriving on the beaches of the area laden with coal, culm and lime. The bustle of activity that surrounded the arrival of a coastal sailing vessel was considerable; indeed, it was something of an occasion for the entire community as the village's casual labour force was turned out to help in the process of *arllwys y llong* – unloading the vessel. By October, these vessels would be laid up for the winter and their crews would then turn their attention to harvesting the bountiful shoals of herring that gathered in Cardigan Bay each autumn. Working from twenty-foot open boats, crews of six or eight men either set nets at specified locations or drifted with the tide with nets in tow. The arrival of the herring boats back on the beaches was also an important communal event, as women and children turned out to help drag the boats clear of the high tide, pick the fish from the nets and carry the catch away. By Christmas the herring fishing season was over and the maintenance of vessels and nets provided employment until the coasters once more set sail in the spring.[1]

It can be seen, therefore, that seafaring was not merely an occupation for the people of Southern Ceredigion, but rather a way of life that actively involved entire communities along the coast. It was, moreover, a way of life that contrasted sharply with that of agricultural communities inland; though much of the trade of the little ports supplied an agricultural market, the two communities had little else in common, economically or socially. The inhabitants of Aber-porth, for instance, described themselves as *pobol Aber-porth* – the people of Aber-porth; though they lived in what was essentially a rural area, they certainly did not consider themselves to be *pobol y wlad* – people of the countryside. The outlook and ambitions of the inhabitants of the coastal communities were entirely orientated towards the sea and as the coastal trade declined gradually from the 1860s onwards, it was only natural for the workforce of the area to seek some form of alternative sea-going employment. Thus it was that many seamen from the area found their way by the 1880s to some of Britain's major ports, of which the booming coal port of Cardiff and its rapidly-expanding fleet of tramp steamers soon proved to be the most convenient and attractive.

Captain Daniel Jenkins, Tre-saith, with crew members aboard the S.S. Italiana *at Antwerp, 10 July 1905*

Back row

J. Davies	*J.R. Jenkins*	*T.M. Thomas*	*E. Walcott*	*G. Halloran*	?	*J.D. Owens*	*W.N. Lewis*
Aber-porth	*Aber-porth*	*Aber-porth*	*Cardiff*	*Cardiff*		*Aber-porth*	*Moylgrove*
(A.B.)	*(O.S.)*	*(Bosun)*	*(Cook)*	*(Steward)*		*(A.B.)*	*(Third engineer)*

Front row

R. Jones	*H. Jones*	*D. Jenkins*	*E.W. Cooke*	*E.R. Roberts*
Aberaeron	*Nefyn*	*Tre-saith*	*Newport (Mon.)*	*Holyhead*
(Second mate)	*(First mate)*	*(Master)*	*(First engineer)*	*(Second engineer)*

A similar shift could be discerned in maritime communities throughout the British Isles during this period as the shipping trade of their local ports declined. Hundreds of mariners from the West Country sought employment at Cardiff with companies founded by their kinsmen such as John Cory, W.J. Tatem and William Reardon Smith. Natives of the coastal communities of Llŷn and Anglesey joined Liverpool companies founded by North Walians such as Robert Thomas of Cricieth and William Thomas of Llanrhuddlad, Anglesey; many also joined the famous Holt Blue Funnel Line, often nick-named 'the Welsh navy' because of the high proportion of Welshmen among its crews. Glasgow became a mecca for the seamen of the West of Scotland, while mariners from the smaller towns and villages on the coast of North-East England turned their attention to tramp shipping companies such as those established by Walter Runciman or Robert Ropner on the Tyne and the Tees. Thus the shift in employment from coastal and short-sea voyages to ocean-going trade evident in the movement of sailors from Southern Ceredigion to Cardiff was being repeated in similar patterns all over Britain, so that by the early twentieth century, the merchant fleet of one of the world's premier industrial countries was, to a considerable degree, manned by men from some of its most remote, non-industrialised areas.

The availability of this new form of maritime employment was to have an important effect upon the coastal communities of Southern Ceredigion, for the vast majority of the mariners who took berths on board the tramp steamers did not move to the ports (such as Cardiff or Barry) from which they now sailed, preferring to retain their homes in their native area. The sea, therefore, continued to provide employment for the menfolk of the coastal communities at a time when the population of Ceredigion as a whole was being depleted by migration to *y gweithe* – the industrial communities of Glamorgan and Monmouth. Whereas the population of Ceredigion fell from over 95,000 in 1881 to 59,042 in 1911 – a loss of over a third of the county's population – the population of the coastal communities remained far more stable.[2]

The relative stability of the population of the coastal towns and villages at the turn of the century was, however, purely nominal. During the mid-nineteenth century, the mariners of these communities had been at home throughout the winter months fishing for herring and repairing boats and nets; moreover, they were absent only for periods of some ten to twelve days during the coastal trading of the spring and summer months. This way of life was largely brought to an end as the sailors of the area turned their attention to deep-sea voyages on Cardiff's tramp steamers during the latter decades of the nineteenth century. At any one time during the year, as great a proportion as two-thirds of the male population of villages such as Aber-porth or Llangrannog might be away on voyages of up to five months to the Black Sea or the River Plate. This affected the seasonal routine of life in the coastal villages in a number of ways. By the eve of the First World War the once important herring fishery of Cardigan Bay had declined considerably[3] and there can be little doubt that this was at least partly due to the fact that there were so few sailors at home during the autumn fishing season. Furthermore, with the decline of herring fishing and coastal trading, there was a sense in which the coastal communities were no longer so intimately associated with the sea and its activities. The communal co-operation and tremendous excitement aroused by the arrival of a coasting smack or the return of the herring fleet were becoming things of the past by 1914 and families whose sea-going husbands and sons had once sailed from beaches a stone's throw from their homes had to be content with tracing the voyages of their relatives in the pages of the *Shipping Gazette* or *Lloyd's List* (both delivered to Aber-porth at that time and paid for by subscriptions from local mariners)[4] as they sailed across the Mediterranean and the Atlantic on board Cardiff's tramp steamers.

But if the old order was changing, the coastal trade had, nevertheless, provided the mariners of Southern Ceredigion with a school of seamanship second to none. Though the ships were small and their cargoes rarely of more than some fifty tons, the handling of such vessls while sailing in confined and shallow channels, or beating away from a beach into the teeth of a stiff South-Westerly demanded a standard of seamanship which Aled Eames has described as '. . . resolute, skilled and courageous'.[5] Most of the sailors from the area who served with Jenkins, Williams & Co. and later with Jenkins Bros., had first gone to sea on board the local sailing coasters. The late Captain Griffith Thomas of Aber-porth went to sea in 1897 as a deck hand on the ketch *Margaret Anne,* owned at Tre-saith; he then served in a similar capacity on board the Jenkins's ketch, *James* and as an A.B. on board the well-known Liverpool ship *Celtic Race* before he became second mate on the Jenkins Bros. tramp, S.S.*Rowtor* in 1905. He later served as second mate on Daniel Jenkins's S.S.*Kingsland.*[6] Others had actually owned coastal trading vessels; due to the decline in the coastal trade towards the turn of the century, the author's great-grandfather, Captain David Jenkins, 'Pen-parc', Aber-porth, sold his ketch *Florrie* in 1899 and obtained a post with the locally-founded shipping company as master of the S.S.*Straits of Menai* in 1900.[7]

The coastal trade had contributed greatly, therefore, to the rich fund of maritime experience and knowledge among the seamen of Southern Ceredigion and it was only natural that James and David Jenkins should have chosen mariners from their native area whom they knew and trusted to captain their vessels in the early years of the firm's history. The first master of the S.S.*Gathorne* was Captain Simon Thomas, 'Glasfor', Aber-porth, who already had experience as master of some of Radcliffe's early tramp steamers behind him when he joined the new company early in 1897. By 1905, three of the four vessels owned by Jenkins Bros. were captained by master mariners from Aber-

The author's great-grandfather, Captain David Jenkins, 'Penparc', Aberporth, enjoying a few moments' relaxation on board the S.S.Farringford, c.1908

porth, as, aptly enough, was Daniel Jenkins's S.S.*Aberporth*. From the turn of the century onwards, there was a steady flow of young men from Aber-porth and nearby communities joining Jenkins Bros. vessels, many of whom were the sons of master mariners who already served with the company. Having become master of the S.S.*Straits of Menai* in 1900, for instance, Captain David Jenkins obtained berths for each of his three sons, John Rees, Samuel and David on various tramp steamers belonging to the company between 1904 and 1911. This was a process actively encouraged by James Jenkins; it was said of him in his obituary that he was

> '. . . unsparing in his efforts to obtain for young men, especially those of his native place, opportunities to begin their careers.'[8]

Equally important in the process of recruiting young men from Southern Ceredigion with their eyes on a career at sea was the part played by Miss Anne Jenkins, James Jenkins's sister, who remained in the family home at Fron-dêg, Aber-porth. Her imposing house set above the beach was often a busy recruiting centre where arrangements were made for teenage boys from the area to join one of the company's tramp steamers for their first deep-sea voyage. It was not unusual, therefore, to find that a considerable proportion of the crew of any of the company's tramp steamers came from the maritime communities of Southern Ceredigion, and as the companies never owned more than some four or five steamers at any one time during most of their history, the Jenkins brothers were personally acquainted with (and in some cases, related to) many of their employees, creating a situation which would have been unusual in a larger company. For example, Mr. Frank Chagnon of Aber-porth recalled an occasion after he and S.R. Davies of Cwm-cou were discharged from different vessels at Barry in 1914, when they were given a lift home to West Wales with Mrs. Jane Jenkins, who was on her way to visit her sister Anne at Aber-porth in the chauffer-driven Rolls Royce owned by the Jenkinses! Such familiarity between the deckhand and an engineer on one hand and the wife of one of the managing owners on the other would have been unthinkable in most shipping companies at the time![9]

The Jenkinses did not rely exclusively upon mariners from their native area, however; a large number of masters and officers employed by the company were from North-West Wales, an area whose sea-faring traditions were as deeply-rooted as those of the coastal communities of Ceredigion. In the early days, it would appear that the influence of W.J. Williams brought some North Walian masters into the company, notably Captain E.T. Elias who came from Williams's native village of Bethesda and who stayed with Williams as master of the S.S.*Straits of Menai* after he left James Jenkins in 1904. Many of those from North Wales who served with Jenkins Bros. had first come to Cardiff to serve on board the vessels of Owen and Watkin Williams, two brothers from Edern near

Crew members on board the S.S.Glamorgan at Ibiza in 1913. The teenage boy kneeling behind the right-hand lifebelt is Frank Chagnon of Aber-porth on his first deep-sea voyage

Nefyn in the Llŷn Peninsula who, in 1899, established what grew to be a substantial Cardiff tramp shipping company. Captain Hugh Jones of Nefyn, who became master of the S.S.*Italiana* in 1905 and master of the S.S.*Glamorgan* in 1908, for instance, had served as second and first mate on a number of the Williams brothers' vessels, as had Captain D.R. Jones, a native of Caernarfon who became master of the first S.S.*Merioneth* in 1916. Others had moved to steam from the fleets of sailing vessels owned by North Walian companies in Liverpool and elsewhere. Captain E.M. Roberts, a native of Cricieth who was master of the S.S.*Farringford* in 1913, for instance, had served as second and first mate on a number of Porthmadog-owned vessels around the turn of the century. [10]

Well over three quarters of the masters who served with Jenkins Bros. were natives of West and North Wales, as were the overwhelming majority of their officers. Welsh was their first language and it was the natural medium of daily conversation on the company's tramp steamers the world over. Most had an adequate grasp of the English language, but English was reserved for commands on board and business ashore. The author's great-grandfather, Captain David Jenkins, 'Pen-parc', Aber-porth passed away the long hours at sea writing poetry in both languages under the bardic name of *'Morfab'* (son of the sea) and sent some of his compositions to J. Ifano Jones to be considered for publication in the Welsh column that he edited in the *South Wales Weekly*

News.[11] Others, however, were not so certain of their grasp of the English language. When W.B. Jenkins, a native of Solfach and bosun of the S.S.*Powis,* was called upon to give evidence at the inquiry into the loss of that vessel, held at Cardiff in August 1907, he began his deposition by telling the court that he would give his evidence as well as he could in English, even though he could express himself better in Welsh.[12] So pervasive was the use of Welsh in daily conversation on board the company's tramp steamers that Mr. Frank Chagnon of Aber-porth recalled a number of coloured firemen from Butetown who became quite competent Welsh speakers after serving on board tramp steamers owned by Welsh-founded Cardiff companies, such as Jenkins Bros., Radcliffe's, Owen and Watkin Williams and John Mathias's Cambrian Steam Navigation Co.[13]

There was, therefore, a close nucleus of Welsh speakers among the crews of many Jenkins vessels and these men took with them to sea the practices and traditions of Welsh Nonconformity, then at the pinnacle of its influence upon the people of Wales. Among the 241 members of *Yr Hen Gapel,* one of the two Calvinistic Methodist chapels in Aber-porth in 1902, there were twenty-seven master mariners alone, without including officers and seamen.[14] Blaenannerch, two miles inland from Aber-porth, was one of the seminal centres of the religious revival that swept through Wales in 1904-05 and there can be little doubt that many seamen from Southern Ceredigion and other parts of Wales were deeply religious men. In an occupation where men were continually exposed to the wrath of the elements, it was only natural that many were attracted to the Christian religion and the spiritual comfort that it could provide at times of danger. Many master mariners were temperate, chapel-going men who held Sunday school classes and *ysgol gân* – hymn singing practices – aboard their vessels. A sea-faring life, however, took mariners beyond the reach of institutionalised worship, far away from the strict moral influence of the minister, the chapel and the *seiat.* Mariners from Aber-porth, whose shadows would never have darkened the doorway of the *Ship* or the *White Lion* in their native village, nevertheless enjoyed a modest pre-voyage libation in Butetown pubs such as the *Mountstuart* or the *Ship and Pilot,* where they melted into the great racial *pot pourri* that characterised Cardiff's dockland.

In general, seamen from West and North Wales rarely lingered long in Butetown. If they had some leave due they generally took trains home to their native area as soon as they were paid off, whereas those sailing again within a few days often stayed at 'Welsh' boarding houses such as *Tŷ Hannah Thomas* in James Street, kept by a redoubtable lady of that name from New Quay.[15] Dozens of other boarding houses in Butetown provided temporary homes for seamen and firemen of almost every conceivable race and it was from this ever-changing pool of labour that Cardiff's tramp shipping companies drew the men who kept their ships going at sea. Sailors from Norway, Greece, Spain and

The engineers of the first S.S. Anglesea in 1914, with S.R. Davies of Cwm-cou, the first engineer, seated

Ireland and firemen from India, the West Indies and the Middle East worked together under the command of Welsh officers and engineers on Jenkins Bros. vessels and the crew lists show that desertions at foreign ports were rare. The company had a good name among sailors looking for berths at Cardiff, with a reputation for wholesome food and clean roomy accommodation, especially in the later vessels. Fresh food was served to crews during the duration of a stay in port and while at sea, it was the opinion of Captain Daniel Jenkins, master of the S.S.*Italiana,* that sailors serving with Jenkins Bros.

'. . . were treated better than in most ships as regards to provisions . . .'[16]

Life on board any Cardiff tramp steamer, nevertheless, was tough and uncompromising; of no Cardiff owner could it be said that he over-indulged his crews. A.B.'s earned some £3 to £4 per month in 1913 and for this they worked long hours in all weathers with crew amenities which even in the newer vessels, were crude by present-day standards. While at sea they kept regular watches, four hours on and four hours off, working up to ninety hours each week with no more than four hours rest at a time. Coaldust, grease and sea-water were their constant companions and during rough weather they might be wet through for days, especially if they were at the helm on an open bridge with a flimsy canvas dodger their only protection from the weather. A small stove in the fo'c's'le was the only means of drying their clothes. Much of the work on board was physically arduous and far from pleasant. Taking on coal was a filthy job that shrouded both the crew and their vessel in choking clouds of thick black dust and the subsequent loading of grain at a Black Sea or River Plate port involved the laborious erection of shifting boards in the holds to keep the cargo in place. Even more gruelling was the lot of the firemen in the stokehold. Every day they would shovel some twenty tons of coal into shoulder-high apertures two feet wide, exposed to the fire blazing white-hot in their faces and surrounded by swirling coal dust and the deafening clamour of shovels ringing on the steel plates of the stokehold. Continually at the mercy of such varied elements, it is hardly surprising that accidents sometimes occurred. A young A.B. at the helm of the S.S.*Powis* suffered dreadful facial injuries when he was hurled right over the wheel during a storm in the Mediterranean in June 1902. Medical care after such accidents was rudimentary;

'. . . he was severly wounded in the face, split his lower lip in two; we bandaged him up the best way we could . . .'[17]

wrote Captain Daniel Jenkins, then master of the S.S.*Powis,* of this accident. Even less could be done for serious illnesses; Captain David Jenkins of Aberporth fell into a diabetic coma in mid-Atlantic on his last voyage as master of the S.S.*Cardigan* in November 1910 and despite hospital treatment at Buenos Aires he died on 27 January 1911.[18] Much attention has been given − and quite rightly so − to the atrocious conditions in which coal miners worked in

Captain Herbert Williamson, Cardiff, later of St. Dogmaels

the early decades of the twentieth century, yet it is not often mentioned that as late as 1938, there were still almost three times as many fatalities among Britain's merchant seamen as among its coal miners.[19] Moreover, the problems involved in setting up an effective union organisation among a work-force scattered in small groups all over the world's oceans made it difficult for the seamen to lobby effectively for better working conditions in the early twentieth century.

A sea-faring life also entailed an enforced separation from home and family. There was very little leave and while deck-hands and A.B.'s (who were signed-on for the length of a voyage alone) might enjoy some eight to twelve weeks ashore each year, the service of officers was often retained between voyages. S.R. Davies of Cwm-cou completed his long years of service with James Jenkins as first engineer of the S.S.*Radnor* from August 1923 until the vessel was sold in March 1927; his discharge book shows that he cannot have been at home for more than *fifteen* days during that entire period.[20] In order that they might spend a little more time with their wives, masters were allowed the privilege of bringing their wives aboard while they were discharging grain at ports such as Hamburg or Antwerp, for the short voyage back to Newport, Cardiff or Barry. On 4 July 1905, for instance, Captain Daniel Jenkins wrote to James Jenkins from Antwerp requesting

'. . . your kind permission to have my wife to stay on board the ship whilst we are here, also for her passage round to the loading port.'[21]

Such periods of conjugal company were but brief interludes in what was otherwise, for the women of the maritime communities, an almost permanent separation from their husbands. It is difficult to fathom the anguish and worry that they must have experienced on countless stormy nights, with the thousands of miles of forbidding seas between them and their loved ones. Such a way of life resulted in these women developing a tremendous strength of character that enabled them to endure the absence of their husbands while bringing up their families single-handed. The sea was just as much a way of life to them as it was to their sea-faring menfolk.

Despite its manifest hardships, the sea continued to be the chief means of livelihood in coastal communities throughout Wales up until the Second World War. For many young men from these areas it was the realisation of a hankering ambition that they had nurtured throughout their childhood as they saw their fathers, uncles and elder brothers leaving home to join their ships and returning with presents and stories from faraway places. To deny this admittedly romantic view of sea-faring life would be to mis-represent the recollections of retired seamen who reminisce about their years at sea with an enthusiasm that never lapses into maudlin sentimentality. Nevertheless, behind it all lay a basic economic reality; these men went to sea, not only because they knew no other

Captain T.L. Davies, Dinas Cross

way of life by the latter decades of the nineteenth century, but because there was no other form of employment available. For almost three-quarters of a century, therefore, mariners from Southern Ceredigion, among those from other Welsh coastal areas, manned the tramp steamers that exported the 'black gold' of South Wales to all parts of the world. Steaming slowly but surely across the Mediterranean and the Atlantic at some seven knots, theirs was a manner of sea-faring that lacked the grossly exaggerated romance of sailing ships battling around the Horn, or the impressive glamour of the great ocean liners, but without them, a world that moved entirely upon the calorific power of South Wales steam coal would have ground to a halt. They were as much a lynchpin in the economic fabric of the world during the Victorian and Edwardian eras as were the colliers of the Rhondda and it is strangely inconsistent that so much attention should have been paid to the latter when so little has been recorded and written about the seamen who manned Cardiff's tramp steamers.

CHAPTER 7

Jenkins Bros., 1914-1920

In his *English History, 1914-1945,* the eminent historian A.J.P. Taylor described the role of British shipowners during the First World War as being that of both profiteers and patriots.[1] The demand for ships increased substantially and there was an unprecedented advance in freight rates that exceeded anything that the oldest shipowners could remember; in 1910 it cost no more than eighteen shillings per ton to ship coal from Cardiff to the River Plate, but by 1916 the maximum rate was £3-17-6d per ton and this figure had doubled again by 1918.[2] Similarly, the rate per ton for shipping coal from Cardiff to Port Said rose from seven shillings in 1913 to £6 in 1917.[3] This tremendous increase in freight rates throughout the war was exacerbated by a deficiency in carrying capacity brought about by enemy action. Although profit margins were high, British shipowners suffered heavy losses in tonnage before Lloyd George imposed the convoy system on a reluctant Admiralty in mid-1917. Before that date losses were enormous; from April to September 1915, 580,000 gross tons of British shipping was lost (half as much again as the shipyards could build during that period), while in April 1917 alone, 870,000 gross tons of shipping was destroyed, chiefly by U-boats.[4]

From the outbreak of war any British merchant vessel was liable to requisition by the government. An owner whose vessel was requisitioned, or whose vessel was carrying a cargo on government account, was paid the 'Blue Book' rates, which were substantially lower than those obtainable on the open market. This was naturally the bone of much contention, especially when the government took over much of the maritime insurance arrangements for the duration of the war. Compensation was based upon an estimate of future earnings based upon the 'Blue Book' rates and because of this, the sum paid often fell short of replacements costs at that time. Despite their general dislike of the concept of government intervention, there was little that the shipowners could do about it. They remained responsible for manning and repairs, but they often had no voice in deciding the employment of their vessels when requisitioned, so much so that they sometimes did not know their whereabouts nor their destinations.[5]

These then were the circumstances in which James and David Jenkins, among hundreds of other shipowners throughout Britain's major ports, had to operate during the war years. During the first months of the war ships in British ports were those most likely to be requisitioned, and early in August 1914 the S.S.*Cardigan,* recently returned from Rotterdam to Barry in ballast, was taken over by the government on an Admiralty charter. Her relief master at the time, Captain T.L. Davies of Dinas Cross, sailed from Barry with a cargo of coal on 7 August 1914; his destination was given to him in a packet of sealed orders which was not to be opened until he was in a position approximately twenty miles north of St. Ives in Cornwall. Having opened the orders, Captain Davies discovered that his cargo was bound for naval bunkers at Portsmouth and thereafter, in the late summer and early autumn of 1914, the S.S.*Cardigan* was regularly employed on the transport of steam coal from Barry to both Portsmouth and Devonport.[6] On each occasion Captain Davies had no idea of his destination until he was well down the Bristol Channel.

Later that autumn the S.S.*Cardigan* was released from the Admiralty charter and she sailed from Barry on 14 October with a cargo of coal for Portland, Oregon; during the outward voyage she is said to have been the first British-registered vessel to traverse the newly-opened Panama Canal.[7] She returned to Europe with a cargo of grain for Naples, where she docked on 16 March 1915; here her crew learnt that their vessel had been sold three days previously to the Greek shipowner N.D. Lykiardopulo of Piraeus for £44,459. The reasons behind the sale are not clear, for any ship at sea during the early years of the war was a guaranteed source of profit, as long as she was not requisitioned. Nevertheless, the S.S.*Cardigan* had completed eight years' service for the firm and in the inflated shipping prices of wartime she had been sold at a profit in excess of £16,000 after depreciation. Her sale left the Cardigan Steamship Co. with one vessel, the S.S.*Anglesea* and in July 1915 an extraordinary general meeting of the company was held to revise its financial arrangements. The capital of the company was increased by £65,000 to £100,000, divided into 100,000 shares at £1 each, while the reserve fund of the company was distributed to the original shareholders as shares in the new capital. The new shareholders' list also showed the way in which James and David Jenkins, both as individuals and as Jenkins Bros., were buying up a large number of shares in the Cardigan Steamship Co. than had ever been the case before in any of their single-ship companies. As the companies became more profitable, especially during the buoyant conditions of the First World War, it paid managing owners to buy blocks of shares in their companies as they became available and this policy was pursued by other Cardiff owners such as Evan Thomas, Radcliffe & Co. during this period.[8]

The substantial profits made by Cardiff shipowners, especially during the first two years of hostilities, are reflected in the balance sheets of the single-ship companies managed by Jenkins Bros. Between 1911 and 1916 an overall loss of £876-7-0d by the Italiana Steamship Co. was transformed into a nett profit in excess of £23,000, while between 1910 and 1916 the Rowtor Steamship Co. transformed a loss of £1,250 into a nett profit of £25,000. Similarly, in their balance sheets of March 1916, the Harrogate and Cardigan Steamship Cos. showed respective nett profits of £17,800 and £29,000. The profits on individual voyages were sometimes enormous; three 'open voyages' by the S.S.*Anglesea* in 1915 revealed a trading profit in excess of £50,000. Dividends paid to shareholders during the war years were good and while there is, unfortunately, very little information available on the sums paid to shareholders in the Jenkins Bros. companies, it is known that the Cardigan Steamship Co. paid 10% dividends in 1915 and 1916 and the Rowtor Steamship Co. paid dividends of not less than 8½% throughout the war.[9]

The enormous profits being made, however, led to considerable public unease about 'war profiteering' and in September 1915 an Excess Profits Duty was introduced as part of the Finance Act.[10] This made provision for a duty of 50% to be imposed upon any increase in pre-war profits and it was increased to 80% in 1917. Its effect on profits was marked; in March 1918, for instance, the profits of the Cardigan Steamship Co. were only a third of what they had been twelve months previously and this decrease was compounded by the fact that all British merchant ships were being paid 'Blue Book' rates only by that date. Within the first year of its operation the Excess Profits Duty revealed a revenue in excess of £100 m. and some major tramp shipowners, notably Edward Nicholl of Cardiff, disposed of their fleets rather than pay what they considered to be an extortionate tax. Possibly in an attempt to alleviate some of the effects of this new tax it would appear that sometime in 1915 James and David Jenkins set up a company called The Celtic Shipping & Insurance Co. No ships were ever registered in this company's name and while it is not clear to what degree (if at all) it was involved in maritime insurance, it would appear that its chief purpose was to siphon off some of the profits of the single-ship companies and subsequently to invest these profits by purchase of shares in those same companies. Thus by February 1917 the Celtic Shipping & Insurance Co. held 20,000 shares in the Carmarthen (formerly Rowtor) Steamship Co. The firm appears never to have been registered at Companies' House and was probably wound up soon after the end of the war.

At the end of 1915 the Jenkins Bros. fleet was still intact, having suffered no losses, nor even any attacks, though this fortunate situation was destined to change entirely during 1916. On 11 January 1916 the S.S.*Farringford* was northward bound for Garston, near Liverpool, with a cargo of copper ore from Huelva in Spain when she was captured by the German auxiliary cruiser *Möwe*. Her crew was taken aboard the German vessel, all destined to remain as prisoners of war until hostilities ceased in 1918 and the S.S.*Farringford* was then sunk by gunfire. She was the first of eight vessels sunk by the *Möwe* in the Western Approaches during that month. In July 1916 the S.S.*Anglesea*, commanded by Captain Herbert Williamson, was attacked by gunfire from a U-boat on the surface in the Mediterranean. Captain Williamson returned fire with the gun mounted on the poop of his vessel and in the ensuing skirmish the S.S.*Anglesea* made good her escape. A month later the S.S.*Italiana* also succeeded in fighting off another U-boat cruising on the surface in the Mediterranean, but the latter vessel met her end on 14 September 1916 when

*The S.S.*Glamorgan *under repair at the Barry Commercial Dry Dock,*
14 April 1915

she was torpedoed and sunk 112 miles east of Malta. None of the crew was lost. At the time she was on government charter, sailing from Spain to Salonika with a cargo of hay to feed the mules that were the mainstay of army transport in the revived campaign in that area at the time.

Two replacement vessels were ordered almost immediately and it is indicative of the vastly improved financial situation of the firm that no mortgages were needed to finance the purchases of the new steamers bought in 1916 and 1917. Both vessels were built by William Gray's West Hartlepool yard and the first of them was ordered for the Harrogate Steamship Co. in place of the S.S.*Farringford* in March 1916. The S.S.*Merioneth,* as she was eventually named, was already under construction when the order was placed; she was a steel screw steamer of 3,004 gross tons and she was delivered to Cardiff late in May that year at a cost of £87,500. This substantial sum demonstrates the inflationary spiral that affected all aspects of the shipping industry during the war; whereas the first S.S.*Cardigan* had cost £5-12-6d per deadweight ton in the depressed conditions prevailing in 1907, the smaller S.S.*Merioneth* cost £17-10-0d per deadweight ton nine years later. After the loss of the S.S.*Italiana* later in 1916 James and David Jenkins turned once more to Gray's and on 10 November that year they purchased a new steel screw steamer of 4,262 gross tons which had been launched on 14 July as the S.S.*Arlington* for Henry Samman & Co. of Hull. The latter company had agreed a purchase price totalling £63,950 for the vessel, though it is not known what Jenkins Bros. paid for her when she was made over to them and re-named S.S.*Carmarthen*.[11] The new steamer was not taken over by the Italiana Steamship Co., however. Following their war losses it would appear that Jenkins Bros. wished to rationalise their single-ship companies and in February 1917, the Rowtor Steamship Co. was re-named the Carmarthen Steamship Co. and its capital was increased to £100,000 in £1 shares to take account of its increased assets in wartime. The new company still owned the S.S.*Glamorgan* and it also took control of 32/64ths of the S.S.*Carmarthen;* the other 'half' of the vessel would appear to have been owned directly by James and David Jenkins as Jenkins Bros.

In December 1916 the British shipping industry was brought even more closely under governmental control with the creation of a Ministry of Shipping headed by a Shipping Controller, Sir Joseph Maclay. The system of requisitioning vessels as they were required by the government was terminated and henceforth *all* British merchant ships were requisitioned at 'Blue Book' rates, a decision that further reduced the profitability of many companies during the latter years of the war. Among other duties the Shipping Controller was also made responsible for the allocation, among British owners, of captured enemy vessels and vessels being built in British yards for foreign owners. To all intents and purposes British merchant shipping was 'nationalised' for the remainder of the war and for some years afterwards.

Early the following year the shipping industry faced its most severe test of the entire war as the Germans renewed a campaign of unrestricted submarine warfare. Allied shipping losses in the spring of 1917 amounted to well over a million gross tons and between April and July that year Jenkins Bros. lost their three most modern vessels. On 24 April the S.S.*Anglesea* was torpedoed and sunk 160 miles west of the Scilly Isles, fortunately without loss of life. Some six weeks later on 3 June the S.S.*Merioneth* was captured by a surface-cruising U-boat 105 miles north-west of Tromso in Norway; the crew was taken off and the year-old steamer sunk by gunfire. Finally, on 26 July the S.S.*Carmarthen* was torpedoed and sunk (again without loss of life) two miles south-east of the Lizard in Cornwall. At the beginning of August 1917 only the S.S.*Glamorgan* remained afloat under Jenkins Bros. colours.

*The second S.S.*Anglesea *was completed by Gray's of West Hartlepool in November 1917 (World Ship Photo Library)*

Despite rising prices James and David Jenkins were not slow to order replacement tonnage. Following the loss of the first S.S.*Anglesea* they ordered a second shelter-decked steamer of almost identical dimensions from the same builders, Richardson, Duck & Co. of Stockton-on-Tees. Delivered to Cardiff in October 1917, she was named S.S.*Cardigan* in place of her predecessor sold in 1915 and became the property of the Cardigan Steamship Co. A month later a further tramp steamer of 4,460 gross tons, the second S.S.*Anglesea,* was delivered from William Gray's West Hartlepool yard. She had been ordered originally by the well-known London shipping firm, F.C. Strick & Co., but by an agreement of July 1917, they disposed their interest in the contract to Jenkins Bros. as managers of the Cardigan Steamship Co. In the original contract the

73

price of the vessel was stated to be £147,500; this worked out at £18-10-0d per deadweight ton, indicating the continuing upward trend in the price of new tonnage during the war. The fleet managed by Jenkins Bros. was further augmented in 1917 by two vessels allocated to the firm by the Shipping Controller. The first was the S.S.*Huntshead*, a steel screw steamer of 3,779 gross tons, completed by Richardsons, Westgarth & Co. in 1901 as the S.S.*Korana* for a firm based at Fiume near Trieste. Taken as a prize early in 1917, she was allocated to Jenkins Bros. that year and re-named with the 'Hunt' prefix, as were a number of captured vessels taken over by the Shipping Controller. The second vessel was the S.S.*Daghlid*, which at 7,979 gross tons, was the largest vessel ever managed by Jenkins Bros. She had been ordered by a Norwegian company late in 1915, but upon her completion by Doxfords of Sunderland in 1916, she spent a brief period with Glover Bros. of London before being allocated to Jenkins Bros. in 1917. Unlike the S.S.*Huntshead*, however, which remained under Jenkins Bros. management until 1921, the S.S.*Daghlid* was transferred to the management of G. Heyn & Sons, Belfast in 1918.

Despite the battering that they had received during the war, from both enemy action and the government's fiscal policies, the cessation of hostilities in November 1918 saw the single ship companies managed by Jenkins Bros. in exceptionally strong financial circumstances. The assets of the Cardigan Steamship Co., had grown from under £50,000 in 1912 to over £131,000 in 1918, while those of the Carmarthen (formerly Rowtor) Steamship Co. had increased from a little over £41,000 in 1913 to £149,000 in 1918. Both companies had extensive cash reserves in the bank and had large sums invested in war bonds and loans; the Cardigan Steamship Co., for instance, had an investment of over £24,000 in war bonds in 1918.

The immediate post-war period was characterised by a remarkable shipping boom throughout Britain, whose effects were especially noticeable at Cardiff. It came about as a result of a number of factors; there was a shortage of available tonnage caused both by war-time losses and dislocation at the ports, while there was also an increased demand for coal on the continent after the ravages of war had temporarily halted production in the important coalfields on the Franco-Belgian border. With freight rates still high, total newcomers to the shipping industry (many of whom it was said, '. . . didn't know one end of a ship from the other') indulged in feverish speculation, buying up substantial fleets at grossly inflated prices. One of the most spectacular examples of such reckless buying came late in 1919, when Edgar Edwards of Llandaf (who prior to the boom had owned no more than four elderly tramp steamers dating from the 1890s) bought Walter Runciman's entire 'Moor Line' fleet at a price in excess of £1.8 m.[12]

Cardiff's older-established shipowners generally shunned the spiralling inflationary boom in which the newcomers were so avidly participating, though

The second S.S.Cardigan about to discharge a cargo of grain from the River Plate at Manchester docks, August 1919

some, such as W.J. Tatem, made enormous profits by selling off their fleets at prices in excess of £20 per deadweight ton. James and David Jenkins also took advantage of the high prices being fetched by shipping tonnage when they sold the S.S.*Glamorgan* in 1919 to the Marga Steamship Co. Her sale price is not known, but in the prevailing market of the period, it was probably in the region of £100,000. Thus, of the five single-ship companies managed by Jenkins Bros. at the end of 1919, only one, the Cardigan Steamship Co., still owned tonnage, in the form of the two 1917-built steamers, S.S.*Cardigan* and S.S.*Anglesea*. Despite the fact that freight rates remained relatively high in 1919-20, the partners realised that it would be foolish to purchase new tonnage for the other four companies with prices so inflated. From March 1919 onwards, therefore, the rationalisation of the firm's activities continued with the winding-up of the obsolete companies. The first two to go were the Harrogate Steamship Co. and the Italiana Steamship Co., both wound-up on 29 March 1919; James and David Jenkins awarded themselves the substantial sum of £33,000 as compensation for loss of management and the remainder of the assets of the two companies was distributed among the shareholders. For every £1 that they had invested shareholders in the Harrogate Steamship Co. received £4-17-10d, and shareholders in the Italiana Steamship Co. received £3-10-6d.[13] One shareholder in the latter company, a Lancashire cotton master who had set up in business near Moscow in the 1890s, had returned destitute after the revolution of 1917 and was understandably delighted to discover that a sum of some hundreds of pounds was due to him from his investment made seventeen years previously.[14]

Later in 1919 the partners turned their attention to the winding-up of the Carmarthen (formerly Rowtor) Steamship Co. Investors in the Rowtor Steamship Co. had, in 1917, already received £2-19-4d for each £1 invested; with the winding-up of the Carmarthen Steamship Co., completed on 21 November 1919, they received a further £1-19-7d. Shortly afterwards, however, on 29 November, David Jenkins died at the relatively early age of 59 years while on a visit to his cousin, Miss Anne Jenkins at Fron-dêg, Aber-porth and he was interred in the graveyard at St. Cynwyl's Church, Aber-porth on 4 December 1919. He had no surviving children; his only daughter, Annie Mary, had died aged 18 years in June 1907 and he predeceased his father, Captain Griffith Jenkins, who was 86 years old at the time of his son's death. In his will, proved on 20 March 1920, David Jenkins left the substantial sum of £119,469-2-2d, reflecting the considerable profitability of the firm during the war years.[15] With his death the fifteen year-old partnership of Jenkins Bros. was brought to an end and James Jenkins's preoccupation in the early months of 1920 was to be the creation of a new managing partnership to continue the operation of the firm's tramp steamers.

CHAPTER 8

James Jenkins, Sons & Co., 1920-1927

As a result of the death of David Jenkins in November 1919, a new managing company was formed in January 1920 under the title of James Jenkins, Sons & Co. Ltd. The new firm comprised 20,000 £1 shares divided between its three managing directors; James Jenkins, the senior partner, held 12,000 of these shares and his eldest son, Hugh J.S. Jenkins, then recently graduated from Oxford, held a further 4,000. The remaining shares were all held by William Walker Chamberlain who had joined the firm as an office boy after he left school in 1900. Having been excused from military service on medical grounds during the First World War, his twenty years of unbroken service with the firm had made him thoroughly conversant with all aspects of tramp shipping management and it was he who handled much of the routine business of the firm, especially during those periods when James Jenkins was away at the country residence at Llandrindod Wells that he purchased in 1920. The new firm retained the offices in the Merchants' Exchange that had been occupied successively by Jenkins, Williams & Co. and Jenkins Bros. since 1899; here a staff of no more than five – John Ellis, the chartering clerk, a cashier, two typists and an office boy – handled all the administrative work relating to the business. The firm's superintendent engineer over many years, T.F. Appleton, had a separate office at Adelaide House in James Street.[1] Following the establishment of the new managing firm, the partners also decided upon slight changes in their vessels' house colours; instead of plain black funnels, the ships received yellow funnels with a black top, while a new house flag, consisting of a white diamond bearing a red letter 'J' on a blue 'swallow tail' background was also devised. Hull and superstructure colours remained unchanged.

Cardiff's spectacular post-war boom came to an abrupt end during 1920 as freight rates tumbled; whereas it had cost £5 per ton to ship coal from Cardiff to Constantinople in January 1920, a top rate of twenty-five shillings prevailed by December that year. Homeward freight rates also fell; by January 1921, the rates per ton for cereals from the River Plate to Britain were less than a quarter of those prevailing a year before.[2] The effects of the collapse of freight rates were compounded by the disappearance of many pre-war markets for coal, caused by a number of factors such as the advent of oil as fuel, the revival of continental collieries after the war and the swamping of many European markets with German reparation coal. Whereas in 1913, for instance, the ports of South Wales had exported some 2½ million tons of coal to Italy, this trade had all but ceased by the mid-1920s as Italy's fuel needs were fulfilled with German coal. Moreover, the fuel requirements of another formerly important market, South America, were to an ever-increasing degree met by coal from the U.S.A. during the 1920s.[3] In such circumstances, many of the newer shipowners at Cardiff found themselves unable to pay for vessels so recently acquired at grossly inflated prices and the newspapers of the early 1920s were littered with reports of the demise of over-optimistic entrepreneurs who were left bankrupt as they sold their ships for a sixth of the price that they had paid for them during the boom.[4]

In a survey of the state of Cardiff's shipping industry published in 1921 by the London shipping journal, *Syren and Shipping*, the authors were careful to distinguish between, on one hand,

> '. . . newer shipowning concerns which are experiencing difficulties that may perhaps prove to be of an insurmountable nature. . .',

and on the other,

> '. . . local owners . . . particularly those who have been long enough in the business to know that an industry like shipping is peculiarly susceptible to ups and downs of a more or less violent character . . . .'[5]

While many of the newcomers who had sunk vast sums in shipping during the heady euphoria of 1919-1920 found themselves facing financial ruin as the boom collapsed, Cardiff's older-established owners found themselves somewhat better prepared for the slump that descended during the latter half of 1920. Not having squandered vast sums upon new tonnage, James Jenkins and his partners did exceptionally well out of the brief flourish of prosperity; the Cardigan Steamship Co. showed a gross profit of over £110,000 over the twelve months leading up to April 1920.[6] Indeed, so strong was the financial situation of the Cardigan Steamship Co. that on 29 March 1920 an extraordinary general meeting of the company approved that the sum of £150,000 (being the undivided profits of the company) be distributed among the shareholders. This distribution took the form of an issue of bonus shares of £1 each; for each original £1 share held, each shareholder received 1½ bonus shares. This resulted in an increase of the capital of the Cardigan Steamship Co. from £100,000 to £250,000.[7] Six months later the only other remaining single-ship company, the Powis Steamship Co., was wound up. Having not possessed a vessel since June 1907, it had existed solely as an investment company since that date, holding substantial blocks of shares in both the Cardigan and Rowtor (later Carmarthen) Steamship Cos. The distribution of the company's capital between its shareholders returned the sum of £6-9-6d for every £1 invested.

By the late autumn of 1920, therefore, the rationalisation of the single-ship companies that had commenced eighteen months before was completed. Only the Cardigan Steamship Co. remained, owning the S.S.*Cardigan* and the S.S.*Anglesea*, though James Jenkins, Sons & Co. continued to manage the government-owned S.S.*Huntshead* until the cessation of government shipping control in April 1921. The winter of 1920-1921 saw the depression in shipping

*The S.S.*Radnor *was a shelter-decked vessel completed by Richardson, Duck & Co. of Stockton-on-Tees in July 1923 (World Ship Photo Library)*

really beginning to bite, though the partners were quite fortunate during this period as the S.S.*Cardigan* was on a two-year time charter to the French shipping firm, Compagnie Générale Transatlantique of Paris.[8] This time charter had been agreed in the summer of 1919 when freight rates were still high, ensuring two years of profitable trading for the vessel, regardless of fluctuations in the market. Such fortunate time charter agreements helped a number of Cardiff firms in the early 1920s; the infant Graig Shipping Co., for instance, secured a similar time charter late in 1919 which was crucial to the firm's early financial success.[9] Nevertheless, the general outlook at that time could hardly be described as encouraging, with freight rates and the value of tonnage continuing to fall in 1921. It is probable that James Jenkins and W.W. Chamberlain realised at the time that despite the fact that their two steamers were only some four years old, if the depression continued, in time it would be increasingly difficult to make them pay; accordingly it was decided early in 1921 to wind-up the Cardigan Steamship Co. and to dispose of the S.S.*Cardigan* when her time charter terminated in the early autumn of that year.

On 1 April 1921 James Jenkins and W.W. Chamberlain commenced the voluntary liquidation of the Cardigan Steamship Co. and as managers, took the handsome sum of £25,000 as compensation for loss of management. The shareholders, on the other hand, received £1-9-0d for every £1 share that they held at the time of liquidation, though it was estimated that since the inception of the company in 1907, they had received an overall capital return in excess of £6 per £1 share.[10] Moreover, for every £1 that they had invested in the liquidated company, they also received a £1 share in the new Anglesea Steamship Co. established on 1 April 1921 with a capital of £100,000 to operate the S.S.*Anglesea*. Sold to the Anglesea Steamship Co. for £90,000, the S.S.*Anglesea* became the only vessel managed by James Jenkins, Sons & Co. in October 1921 following the sale of the S.S.*Cardigan* to H.W. Renny of Dundee and the sale by the government of the S.S.*Huntshead* to a Hamburg shipping company. The S.S.*Anglesea* continued to trade for a further seven months before she, too, was sold on 25 May 1922 to the Portfield Steamship Co. of Cardiff (managed by W.E. Hinde) who re-named her S.S.*Portgwarra*. Her sale price was £58,410, reflecting the continuing downward trend in the price of tonnage and despite the fact that the Anglesea Steamship Co. showed a profit of £5,519 for the year ending 31 March 1922, it was clear that profit margins had fallen considerably within less than two years after the collapse of the boom.[11]

By June 1922, therefore, James Jenkins was without a ship under his management for the first time since he had ventured into shipowning in 1897. Indeed, it was a period during which a number of Cardiff's older-established firms sold up because of the depression, notably the Cambrian Steam Navigation Co., which disposed of its final vessel, the S.S.*Western* in 1922. James Jenkins, however, had no intention of withdrawing entirely from shipowning at that time; he and W.W. Chamberlain realised that to trade successfully during periods of depression it was necessary to operate large, modern vessels whose repair bills were low and whose greater deadweight capacity enabled considerable economies of scale to be achieved. Accordingly, on 1 November 1922 an order was placed with Richardson, Duck & Co. of Stockton-on-Tees for a new shelter-decked steamer of 4,576 gross tons for the Anglesea Steamship Co. A little larger, but otherwise almost identical with the second S.S.*Cardigan,* the S.S.*Radnor* (as she was eventually named) cost £81,500, which at a little over £10 per deadweight ton, showed how the price of tonnage had slumped as a result of the depression. This was followed on 1 February 1923 by an order placed with William Gray's West Hartlepool shipyard for another tramp steamer of 4,600 gross tons, built to the same 'long bridge deck' design as the second S.S.*Anglesea;* at the slightly cheaper price of £77,750, the S.S.*Merioneth* (as she was eventually known) cost some £9-15-0d per deadweight ton.

Whereas the S.S.*Radnor* was ordered originally for the Anglesea Steamship Co., the S.S.*Merioneth* was ordered directly by James Jenkins, Sons & Co. and this probably because the managing partnership was considering the establishment of a new firm to own and operate both the new vessels. As a result of the considerable loss incurred by the sale of the second S.S.*Anglesea* and also

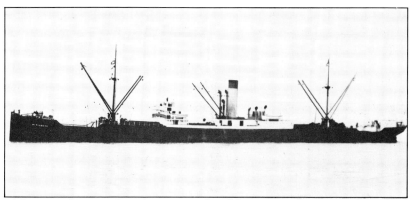

*The second S.S.*Merioneth *was completed by Gray's of West Hartlepool in May 1924 (World Ship Photo Library)*

wishing to avoid the creation of another single-ship company, it was eventually decided to set up a new firm, the Cardigan Shipping Company Ltd. Registered on 22 June 1923, the new company had a capital of £150,000 divided into £1 shares and by an agreement of 29 June, the Anglesea Steamship Co. transferred all its assets, including the S.S.*Radnor,* to the Cardigan Shipping Co. in exchange for 60,000 shares in the new company.[12] The S.S.*Merioneth* was likewise made over to the new company, and in its prospectus, issued in June 1923 the directors, James Jenkins, W.W. Chamberlain and Hugh Jenkins, justified their decision to invest in new tonnage, declaring that

> '. . . even in times of depression, up-to-date vessels carefully managed are more than able to make a profit.'[13]

As directors, they were naturally among the first subscribers to the new company; James Jenkins bought 16,679 shares, W.W. Chamberlain bought 3,406 shares and Hugh Jenkins bought 2,479 shares. A further 13,874 shares were purchased by the managing firm of James Jenkins, Sons & Co. Among the other prominent shareholders were the chandlers Owen and Griffith Hughes, (whose father Evan had bought shares in the Celtic Shipping Co. in 1898), John Morel and John Cory, both members of well-known Cardiff shipping families, Jenkin Jones, the sail and tarpaulin maker and Mrs. W.J. Williams of Barry, the widow of James Jenkins's partner from 1898 until 1904. By October 1923, over 83,000 shares had been allotted, but the initial shareholders' list showed that the sources of capital had altered enormously over the twenty-five years since James Jenkins floated his first shipping companies. Almost two-thirds of the investors in the Cardigan Shipping Co. came from all parts of England, with a particularly strong injection of capital from Cornwall where W.W. Chamberlain had close associations with local shipping enterprises such as the Redruth-based County of Cornwall Shipping Co. Many of the remainder of the investors came from South-East Wales, though in contrast with the shipping companies founded by James Jenkins at the turn of the century, virtually no colliers appeared on the shareholders' lists. With the depression and the wage reductions of the early 1920s, they could ill-afford the luxury of speculative investments in shipping. Those South Walians who invested in the Cardigan Shipping Co. were mostly business and professional people; teachers, lawyers and shopkeepers, who were insulated to a considerable degree from the worst effects of the depression.[14]

The S.S.*Radnor* was delivered to Cardiff in August 1923, though due to delays at Gray's shipyard, the S.S.*Merioneth* did not enter service until the spring of 1924. The combined cost of both those vessels was almost £160,000; their purchase prices were individually secured by personal mortgage loans made to the Cardigan Shipping Co. by James Jenkins himself. James Jenkins had also moved from Penarth into Cardiff that year, to a substantial house in the fashionable suburb of Penylan (he donated his house in Penarth, 'Beecroft', to the local authority, who later used it as a maternity clinic). The entry into service of the S.S.*Radnor* in 1923 coincided with a modest improvement in freight rates, triggered off by a coal strike in the U.S.A. and the French occupation of the Ruhr, Germany's principal industrial area. Nevertheless, this proved to be a short-lived recovery. The 'coal out, grain home' trade that had succoured the wealth of so many Cardiff owners during the pre-war era was disrupted and they now sought cargoes and charters all over the world in order to remain profitable. Between May 1924 and February 1925, for instance, the S.S.*Radnor* under the command of Captain Herbert Williamson, was employed on time charter carrying guano from Nauru Island in the Western Pacific to various Australian ports. In all, the vessel was away for eighteen months and when she returned, T.F. Appleton the superintendent engineer was horrified by the damage caused to the steamer's holds by the obnoxious organic cargo. As for Captain Williamson – always a forthright character – it is said that upon his return, his comments in the office regarding his hot and pungent exile in the Pacific were 'unprintable'.[15]

Just as the S.S.*Radnor* was commencing upon her time charter in the Pacific, James Jenkins and W.W. Chamberlain had decided to wind-up the Anglesea Steamship Co. Since June 1923, the company had existed merely as an investment company with its assets invested in the Cardigan Shipping Co. and it was only logical that the former company should be merged into the latter. Accordingly, the managing company was authorised to distribute the capital of the Anglesea Steamship Co. in specie or in kind, with investors being given the chance to receive two fully paid-up £1 shares in the Cardigan Shipping Co. for every three £1 shares that they held in the Anglesea Steamship Co. Thus, with the winding-up of the Anglesea Steamship Co. and the delivery of the

*The S.S.*Radnor *taking on a cargo of coal at Barry,* c.1925

S.S.*Merioneth* in May 1924, the shipping operation managed by James Jenkins, Sons & Co. assumed the form that it was to retain until James Jenkins's retirement in 1927.

The faith of the managing company that their two new steamers could make a profit despite the depression was borne out on 31 March 1925, with the balance sheet of the Cardigan Shipping Co. showing a profit (albeit modest) of £6,723-11-4d. This enabled a dividend of 6d per share to be paid in May. Nevertheless, the outlook for shipping was still far from bright; the first months of 1925 saw freight rates fall back to pre-war levels while running costs continued to average 50% above pre-war levels. Many Cardiff owners laid up their vessels rather than continue to operate them at a loss, and while the S.S.*Radnor* and the S.S.*Merioneth* were kept fully employed throughout 1925, the financial year ending 31 March 1926 showed a profit of a mere £791-1-9d by the Cardigan Shipping Co. In their report, James Jenkins and W.W. Chamberlain stated that

> '. . . in common with others, this company has felt the effect of the very depressed freight markets. The outlook still remains obscure and it is futile to make prophecies as to the future. The steamers are trading, but the profits are low.'[16]

The beginning of the General Strike shortly afterwards on 3 May 1926 further disrupted the coal trade from South Wales ports, with vessels having to sail out in ballast, though during July and August that year, the S.S.*Merioneth* was one of some ninety vessels to arrive at Cardiff with cargoes of coal from abroad. The miners held out doggedly until they were forced back to work by increasingly desperate poverty on 1 December 1926. For them, the collapse of the strike was a bitter blow, though it was greeted with some optimism by Cardiff's shipowners who foresaw a revival in the port's coal trade with the return to work. One of the foremost in their midst, Lord Glanely (W.J. Tatem) spoke of

> '. . . a revival of activity in South Wales trade . . . the anticipated greatly increased volume of traffic . . .',[17]

but his cheerful outlook belied the losses being sustained by many Cardiff owners as the hoped-for revival largely failed to materialise. By this time, James Jenkins was 66 years old and his three sons, Hugh, Emrys and David, having all been educated at either Oxford or Cambridge, were embarked upon professional careers. None of them had much practical experience in shipping and with the outlook as gloomy as it was early in 1927 James Jenkins decided to retire altogether from shipowning. Accordingly, in March 1927, advantage was taken of a slight rise in tonnage prices following the end of the coal strike and both vessels were sold to Morel Ltd. of Cardiff (the S.S.*Radnor* was re-named S.S.*Treharris* and the S.S.*Merioneth* was re-named S.S.*Aberdare*) for £136,625. This sale price represented a loss of over £18,000, so that despite the

Mr. John Cory presenting an award to Captain Herbert Williamson in October 1927, following his rescue of the crew of a disabled American schooner in mid-Atlantic. Among those looking on is W.W. Chamberlain (second from left in back row)

84

fact that the Cardigan Shipping Co. had made a trading profit of some £12,000 during the year ending on 31 March 1927, the loss written off on the sale of the vessels meant that the company ended up with an overall deficit of £9,570. Finally, in August 1927, shareholders in the Cardigan Shipping Co. received a circular stating that James Jenkins and his son Hugh had resigned as directors in both James Jenkins, Sons & Co. and the Cardigan Shipping Co. Three decades of shipowning and management by the master mariner from Aber-porth were at an end.[18]

Epilogue

Following the resignation of James Jenkins and his son Hugh as directors of the Cardigan Shipping Co. in August 1927, W.W. Chamberlain was joined in the managing partnership by a consortium headed by W.A. Phillips, who owned two coasting colliers at Cardiff. During the following year they purchased four steamers, each of some 2,000 gross tons, which they believed would be better suited to trading conditions at that time. One of these vessels, the S.S.*Marie Llewellyn,* later became famous for her blockade-running exploits during the Spanish Civil War under the command of Captain 'Potato' Jones. W.W. Chamberlain eventually resigned in 1930 and thereafter devoted most of his time to managing the County of Cornwall Shipping Co. in partnership with John Hampton of Redruth. Chamberlain had been associated with that company since 1921 when his wife had launched their first steam coaster, the S.S.*St.Levan* and the firm continued to trade, chiefly from the harbour at Portreath in Cornwall, until the early 1940s.

The Cardigan Shipping Co. thereafter underwent a number of changes of management. In 1937 the company was taken over by Walter T. Gould, whose former partner, J.C. Gould rose to sudden prominence in Cardiff shipping

The first S.S.Cardigan, seen here as the Greek-owned S.S.Athanasios, at Liverpool, c.1920 (World Ship Photo Library)

circles during the boom of 1919-1920, only to crash into bankruptcy six years afterwards. During the Second World War, W.T. Gould managed vessels on behalf of the Ministry of War Transport, but the Cardigan Shipping Co. re-appeared under his management in 1948 and remained so until it was taken over by John Cory & Sons of Cardiff in 1962. At that date the company owned one vessel, the M.V.*Restormel* and she was operated by Cory's until she was sold in 1964. Thereafter the Cardigan Shipping Co. existed in name alone for some years before its assets were bought up by a new consortium formed in 1969. By 1973, the company was jointly managed by Harrisons (Clyde) Ltd., the Blandford Shipping Co. Ltd., Ropner Management Ltd. and Sir Robert Ropner & Co. Ltd.; four bulk carriers and a small ferry were registered in the company's name. Ten years later the *Lloyd's Register List of Shipowners* for 1983-1984 gave the managers of the Cardigan Shipping Co. as Harrisons (Clyde) Ltd. and O. Godager & Co. of Oslo and the vessels registered in the name of the company were the tanker M.V.*Norse Falcon* and the bulk carriers M.V.*Norse Marshall* and M.V.*Norse Pilot*. It is interesting to reflect, therefore, that a direct descendant of the Gathorne Steamship Co. of 1897 has survived into the 1980s and bearing in mind the origins of the company it is appropriate that the two latter vessels were registered at Cardiff.

James Jenkins died at his Cardiff home on 23 February 1940, aged 79 years and was buried at Llandrindod Wells three days later. During his retirement he had shared his time between his homes at Cardiff and Llandrindod Wells and had been the benefactor of numerous charities in both places. Only a year before his death, for instance, he had presented a new operating table to the hospital at Llandrindod Wells where his second son, Dr. Emrys Jenkins, was in medical practice. He left almost £¼ million in his will, a considerable achievement for a man who, at the age of twelve, had gone to sea as a deck boy on an Aber-porth smack, having received only a rudimentary education. Looking back over his career in a letter that he wrote to Captain Herbert Williamson in April 1928, he admitted that his period as a shipowner '. . . had not been without its difficulties and trials . . .', but he felt, nevertheless, that '. . . the past thirty-two years have not been spent in vain . . .'

James and David Jenkins came from a remarkable generation of men from coastal communities throughout Wales, who, as the local coasting trade declined in the late nineteenth century, moved to Cardiff to captain and later (with the opportunities available to enterprising individuals) to own fleets of tramp steamers at that port. During an era when the coal of South Wales was the driving force behind almost every aspect of the world's economy, these steamers were the 'supertankers' of their age. Manned, many of them, by predominantly Welsh crews, they made the names of Cardiff and Wales famous in ports throughout the world. Surprisingly, it is an aspect of the history of our nation that has received relatively little attention, perhaps because man leaves far less

*The last owners of the second S.S.*Cardigan *were the Counties Steamship Management Co. Ltd. of London, who named her S.S.*Bury Hill. *Here she is seen discharging grain in the Roath Dock, Cardiff, shortly before she was wrecked in December 1936*

evidence of his passage across the oceans than across the face of the earth. It is, nevertheless, a fascinating story which historians in Wales have only relatively recently begun to unfold: hopefully this book has provided a record of the part played in that story by James and David Jenkins and the seamen who manned their vessels.

Appendices

Fleet Lists

(The details relating to the *Mary Jane* and the *James* have been taken from the Shipping Registers of the Port of Cardigan; those relating to the steamers are based on information supplied by Mr. Harold Appleyard of the World Ship Society, supplemented by details taken from the Shipping Registers of the Port of Cardiff)

1 The Ceredigion Sailing Coasters

Mary Jane
Official No.: 53435
Wooden smack of 30 gross tons, built in 1868 by John Williams of Netpool, Cardigan for Griffith Jenkins, Dyffryn Mill, Aber-porth.
Length: 53.3 x Beam: 16.4 x Depth/Draught: 6.9 feet.
Foundered and sank on St. Patrick's Causeway, 7 March 1894.

James
Official No.: 29670
Wooden smack of 35 gross tons, built in 1864 by John Williams of Netpool Cardigan for D. Davies, Aber-porth, master mariner and William Stephens of Llechryd, slate merchant.
Length: 53.5 x Beam: 16.5 x Depth/Draught: 7.3 feet.
1873: Transferred to John Stephens of Llechryd, slate merchant.
1882: Purchased by John Jenkins of Fron-dêg, Aber-porth.
1893: Majority shareholding transferred to Miss Anne Jenkins, Fron-dêg.
1894-95: Re-built and re-rigged as a ketch.
1929: Ceased trading.
1937: Declared unseaworthy, 13 August.

2 The Tramp Steamers

These are the managing companies for the following tramp steamers: James Jenkins, 1897, Jenkins, Williams & Co., 1898-1904, Jenkins Brothers, 1904-1920, James Jenkins, Sons & Co., 1920-1927.

Gathorne
In the Fleet: 1897-1901
Official No.: 68148
Tonnage Gross: 1148
Tonnage Nett: 717
Length: 243.9 x Beam: 29.1 x Depth/Draught: 17.5 feet.
Machinery: C.2-cyl. by Greenock Foundry Co., Greenock.
History: 1873: Completed by C. Hill & Sons, Cardiff for C. & E. Hill of Bristol. Later owned by C.O. Young & Christies, Cardiff and W. White, Cardiff. 1878: Sold to Venuesa & Co., Seville, Spain and re-named *Nuevo Ponce*. 1883: Sold to Fisher, Renwick & Co., Newcastle-upon-Tyne, reverting to original name, *Gathorne*. 1.1897: Purchased by Gathorne Steamship Co.Ltd. (J. Jenkins, manager) Cardiff. 2.1898: Transferred to Celtic Shipping Co. Ltd. (Jenkins, Williams & Co., managers). 1901: Sold to J. Raine, Sunderland. 1912: Sold to French shipbreakers and broken up at Boulogne.

North Tyne
In the Fleet: 1898-1904
Official No.: 62358
Tonnage Gross: 1209
Tonnage Nett: 754
Length: 230.0 x Beam: 32.1 x Depth/Draught: 17.3 feet.
Machinery: C.2-cyl. by Blair & Co.Ltd., Stockton-on-Tees.
History; 8.1870: Completed by C. Mitchell & Co., Newcastle-upon-Tyne for W. Dickinson,
Newcastle-upon-Tyne and later owned by H. Robinson, Newcastle-upon-Tyne. 1896: Sold to
J. Whitfield, Newcastle-upon-Tyne. 1896: Sold to G.N. Patterson, Newcastle-upon-Tyne.
1898: Purchased by Celtic Shipping Co.Ltd. (Jenkins, Williams & Co., managers). 1904: Sold
to G.A. Gaponoff, Odessa and re-named *Gregori Gaponoff*. 1910: Sold to W. Wissotzkey &
Co., Odessa. 1913: Sold to Sch. Bedpaloff, Odessa. 8.7.1919: Sunk at Constantinople after
being in collision.

Rowtor
In the Fleet: 1898-1906
Official No.: 98983
Tonnage Gross: 2351
Tonnage Nett: 1511
Length: 288.0 x Beam: 40.0 x Depth/Draught: 18.3 feet.
Machinery: T.3-cyl. by Blair & Co.Ltd., Stockton-on-Tees.
History: 9.1891: Completed by E. Withy & Co., West Hartlepool for J. Holman and Sons,
London. 1898: Purchased by Rowtor S.S. Co.Ltd. (Jenkins, Williams & Co., managers).
11.1904: Management transferred to Jenkins Bros. 3.1.1906: Wrecked on Fratelli Rocks,
Bizerta while on a voyage from Barry to Port Said with a cargo of coal.

Powis
In the Fleet: 1899-1907
Official No.: 96165
Tonnage Gross: 2111
Tonnage Nett: 1331
Length: 275.2 x Beam: 37.9 x Depth/Draught: 19.0 feet.
Machinery: T.3-cyl. by Palmers' Co.Ltd., Newcastle-upon-Tyne.
History; 11.1889: Completed by Palmers' Co.Ltd., Newcastle-upon-Tyne as *County* for
Durham S.S. Co.Ltd. (J. White, manager), Newcastle-upon-Tyne. 1898: Sold to McLaren and
McLaren, Glasgow. 1899: Purchased by Powis S.S. Co.Ltd. (Jenkins, Williams & Co.,
managers) and re-named *Powis*. 11.1904: Management transferred to Jenkins Bros.
20.6.1907: Foundered 25 miles off Seriphos Island while on a voyage from Seriphos to
Middlesborough with a cargo of iron ore.

Straits of Menai
In the Fleet: 1900-1904
Official No.: 104556
Tonnage Gross: 2870
Tonnage Nett: 1849
Length: 314.0 x Beam: 40.5 x Depth/Draught: 21.3 feet.
Machinery: T.3-cyl. by W. Allan & Co., Sunderland.
History: 9.1894: Completed by Furness, Withy & Co.Ltd., West Hartlepool for N. McLean &
Co., Glasgow. 1896: Sold to R.B. Stoker, London and later to British Maritime Trust,
London. 1900: Purchased by Straits of Menai S.S. Co.Ltd. (Jenkins, Williams & Co.,
managers). 9.1904: Management transferred to W.J. Williams & Co., Cardiff. 1906:
Management transferred to Williams and Mordey. 1910: Sold to J. Arvanitidi fils, Greece and
re-named *Chalkydon*. 1913: Sold to Bank of Athens (J. Arvantides fils, manager), Greece.
1916: Sold to J. Arvantides fils, Greece. 14.7.1917: Captured by the German submarine U.15
about 600 miles west of Gibraltar and sunk by gunfire the following day.

Farringford
In the Fleet: 1900-1916
Official No.: 106410
Tonnage Gross: 3146
Tonnage Nett: 1993
Length: 325.0 x Beam: 45.4 x Depth/Draught: 23.7 feet.
Machinery: T.3-cyl. by J. Dickinson & Sons Ltd., Sunderland.
History: 7.1896: Completed by J.L. Thompson & Sons Ltd., Sunderland, for Farringford S.S.
Co.Ltd. (Charlton and Thompson, managers) Sunderland. 1900: Purchased by Harrogate S.S.
Co.Ltd. (Jenkins, Williams & Co., managers). 11.1904: Management transferred to Jenkins
Bros. 11.1.1916: Captured and sunk by the German auxiliary cruiser *Möwe* in a position
44.00N 12.25W while on a voyage from Huelva to Garston with a cargo of copper ore.

Italiana
In the Fleet: 1900-1916
Official No.: 106909
Tonnage Gross: 2663
Tonnage Nett: 1706
Length: 305.5 x Beam: 44.1 x Depth/Draught: 22.5 feet.
Machinery: T.3-cyl. by Hall, Brown, Buttery & Co., Glasgow.
History: 10.1898: Completed by R. Duncan & Co., Port Glasgow for British Maritime Trust,
London. 1900: Purchased by Italiana S.S. Co.Ltd. (Jenkins, Williams & Co., managers).
11.1904: Management transferred to Jenkins Bros. 14.9.1916: Sunk by a German submarine
in a position 36.00N 16.50E while on a voyage from Rocas Bay and Tarragona to Salonica
with a cargo of hay.

Glamorgan
In the Fleet: 1906-1919
Official No.: 123170
Tonnage Gross: 3539
Tonnage Nett: 2258
Length: 342.0 x Beam: 51.0 x Depth/Draught: 22.7 feet.
Machinery: T.3-cyl. by J. Dickinson & Sons Ltd., Sunderland.
History: 10.1906: Completed by Craig, Taylor & Co.Ltd., Stockton-on-Tees for Rowtor S.S.
Co.Ltd. (Jenkins Bros., managers). 1917: Transferred to Carmarthen S.S. Co.Ltd. (same
managers). 1919: Sold to Marga S.S. Co.Ltd. (C. Angel, manager), Cardiff. 1919: Sold to
D.R. Llewellyn, Merrett & Price Ltd. (Merrett Bros. Ltd., managers), Cardiff. 1920: Re-
named *River Wye*. 24.11.1923: Wrecked on Mouton Island while on a voyage from Swansea
to Boston Mass. with a cargo of coal.

Cardigan (1)
In the Fleet: 1907-1915
Official No.: 123184
Tonnage Gross: 4295
Tonnage Nett: 2691
Length: 355.0 x Beam: 51.2 x Depth/Draught: 26.1 feet.
Machinery: T.3-cyl. by North Eastern Marine Engineering Co., Sunderland.
History: 1907: Completed by Ropner & Son, Stockton-on-Tees for Cardigan S.S. Co.Ltd.
(Jenkins Bros., managers), Cardiff. 1915: Sold to N.D. Lykiardopulo, Piraeus and re-named
Athanasios. 1938: Sold to Japanese owners and probably broken up soon afterwards.

Anglesea (1)
In the Fleet: 1914-1917
Official No.: 136939
Tonnage Gross: 4534
Tonnage Nett: 2795
Length: 400.3 x Beam: 52.0 x Depth/Draught: 24.3 feet.
Machinery: T.3-cyl. by Blair & Co.Ltd., Stockton-on-Tees.
History: 7.1914: Completed by Richardson, Duck & Co., Stockton-on-Tees for Cardigan S.S.
Co.Ltd. (Jenkins Bros., managers). 18.7.1916: Attacked by gunfire by an enemy submarine in
the Mediterranean. The *Anglesea* opened fire and escaped. 24.4.1917: Torpedoed and sunk
without warning 160 miles west of Bishops Rock.

Merioneth (1)
In the Fleet: 1916-1917
Official No.: 136985
Tonnage Gross: 3004
Tonnage Nett: 1854
Length: 320.0 x Beam: 46.5 x Depth/Draught: 22.3 feet.
Machinery: T.3-cyl. by Central Marine Engine Works, West Hartlepool.
History: 5.1916: Completed by Wm. Gray & Co.Ltd., West Hartlepool for Harrogate S.S.
Co.Ltd. (Jenkins Bros., managers). 3.6.1917: Captured by a German submarine 105 miles N.
by W. from Tromso and sunk by gunfire.

Carmarthen
In the Fleet: 1916-1917
Official No.: 139598
Tonnage Gross: 4262
Tonnage Nett: 2690
Length: 380.0 x Beam: 51.0 x Depth/Draught: 24.8 feet.
Machinery: T.3-cyl. by Central Marine Engine Works, West Hartlepool.
History: 7.1916: Completed by Wm. Gray & Co.Ltd., West Hartlepool as *Arlington* for H.
Samman & Co. of Hull. 11.1916: Purchased by Jenkins Bros., Cardiff and re-named
Carmarthen. 2.1917: Transferred to Carmarthen S.S. Co.Ltd. (Jenkins Bros., managers),
Cardiff. 26.7.1917: Torpedoed and sunk by a German submarine 2 miles S.E. of The Lizard.

Cardigan (2)
In the Fleet: 1917-1921
Official No.: 139622
Tonnage Gross: 4534
Tonnage Nett: 2781
Length: 400.0 x Beam: 52.0 x Depth/Draught: 32.3 feet.
Machinery: T.3-cyl. by Blair & Co.Ltd., Stockton-on-Tees.
History: 10.1917: Completed by Richardson, Duck & Co.Ltd., Stockton-on-Tees for Cardigan
S.S. Co.Ltd. (Jenkins Bros., managers). 2.1920: Management transferred to J. Jenkins, Sons &
Co. 1921: Sold to H.W. Renny (E.J. Leslie, manager), Dundee. 1924: Sold to Harlem S.S.
Co.Ltd. (Brown, Jenkinson & Co.Ltd., managers), London and re-named *Pensylvanie*. 1926:
Sold to Cie Générale Transatlantique, France. 1934: Sold to Sussex S.S. Co.Ltd. (Counties
S.S. Management Co., managers), London and re-named *Bury Hill*. Wrecked in December
1936.

Anglesea (2)
In the Fleet: 1917-1922
Official No.: 139625
Tonnage Gross: 4460
Tonnage Nett: 2818
Length: 380.3 x Beam: 52.0 x Depth/Draught: 26.0 feet.
Machinery: T.3-cyl. by Central Marine Engine Works, West Hartlepool.
History: 11.1917: Completed by Wm. Gray & Co.Ltd., West Hartlepool for Cardigan S.S.
Co.Ltd. (Jenkins Bros., managers). 2.1920: Management transferred to J. Jenkins, Sons & Co.
1921: Transferred to Anglesea S.S. Co.Ltd. (J. Jenkins, Sons & Co., managers). 1922: Sold to
Portfield S.S. Co.Ltd. (W.E. Hinde & Co. managers), Cardiff and re-named *Portgwarra*.
1933: Sold to New Era S.S. Co.Ltd. (F.S. Dawson, manager), Cardiff and re-named *Thomas
Walton*. 3.12.1939: Torpedoed and sunk by U-boat in position 67.52N, 14.28E.

Radnor
In the Fleet: 1923-1927
Official No.: 145728
Tonnage Gross: 4576
Tonnage Nett: 2798
Length: 400.0 x Beam: 52.0 x Depth/Draught: 24.3 feet.
Machinery: T.3-cyl. by Blair & Co.Ltd., Stockton-on-Tees.
History: 7.1923: Completed by Richardson, Duck & Co.Ltd., Stockton-on-Tees for Cardigan
Shipping Co.Ltd. (J. Jenkins, Sons & Co., managers). 1927: Sold to Gardépée S.S. Co.Ltd.
(Morel Ltd., managers), Cardiff and re-named *Treharris*. 1928: Transferred to Nolisment S.S.
Co.Ltd. (same managers). 1933: Sold to A. Lauro, Naples and re-named *Aida Lauro*.
1.7.1937: Wrecked off Castle Point, St. Just, Cornwall while on a voyage from Bombay to
Hull with general cargo.

Merioneth (2)
In the Fleet: 1924-1927
Official No.: 148272
Tonnage Gross: 4600
Tonnage Nett: 2811
Length: 400.0 x Beam: 52.0 x Depth/Draught: 25.6 feet.
Machinery: T.3-cyl. by Central Marine Engine Works, West Hartlepool.
History: 5.1924: Completed by Wm. Gray & Co.Ltd., West Hartlepool for Cardigan
Shipping Co.Ltd. (J. Jenkins, Sons & Co., managers). 1927: Sold to Lesreaulx S.S. Co.Ltd.
(Morel Ltd., managers), Cardiff and re-named *Aberdare*. 1928: Transferred to Nolisment S.S.
Co.Ltd. (same managers). 1933: Sold to A. Lauro, Naples and re-named *Antonio Limoncelli*.
12.1941: Taken over by the Brazilian Government. 1942: Re-named *Paranaloide*. 1950:
Returned to A. Lauro and re-named *Antonio Limoncelli*. 7.1950: Broken up at La Spezia.

Vessels managed on behalf of the Shipping Controller, 1917-1921.

Huntshead
In the Fleet: 1917-1921
Official No.: 137736
Tonnage Gross: 3779
Tonnage Nett: 2387
Length: 350.0 x Beam: 46.5 x Depth/Draught: 21.2 feet.
Machinery: T.3-cyl. by Richardsons, Westgarth & Co.Ltd., Sunderland.
History: 12.1901: Completed by J. Priestman & Co., Sunderland as *Korana* for Soc. in Azioni
Ungarto Croata per la Nav. Liberia, Fiume. 1917: Taken as a prize at Eleusis, allocated to the
Shipping Controller (Jenkins Bros., managers) and re-named *Huntshead*. 1920: Management
transferred to J. Jenkins, Sons & Co. 1921: Sold to Hamburg Amerika Packetf. A.G.,
Germany. 1922: Sold to Mifsud Bros., Malta and re-named *San Paul*. 1923: Sold to National
S.S. Co. of Malta (C. Mifsud, manager), Malta. 1924: Sold to G. Dacoutros, G. Sorotto,
G. Lykiardopulo and G. Coleiro, Malta and re-named *Aghios Spyridon*. 1933: Broken up in
Italy.

Daghild
In the Fleet: 1917-1918
Official No.: 139160
Tonnage Gross: 7979
Tonnage Nett: 4810
Length: 455.0 x Beam: 58.1 x Depth/Draught: 33.2 feet.
Machinery: T.3-cyl. by the Shipbuilders.
History: 1916: Completed by Wm. Doxford & Sons Ltd., Sunderland for Glover Bros.,
London. 1917: Taken over by the Shipping Controller (Jenkins Bros., managers). 1918:
Management transferred to G. Heyn & Sons. 1920: Sold to A/S Daghild (J.P. Pedersen &
Sons, managers), Norway (originally ordered by this company). 1923: Sold to Tenax S.S.
Co.Ltd. (Muir, Young Ltd., managers). 1936: Sold to W. Kunstmann of Stettin, Germany
and re-named *Katharina Dorothea Fritzen*. Her ultimate fate is not known.

Vessels owned and managed by Daniel Jenkins and associated companies, 1903-1910.

Aberporth
In the Fleet: 1903-1905
Official No.: 89210
Tonnage Gross: 1969
Tonnage Nett: 1231
Length: 270.5 x Beam: 36.8 x Depth/Draught: 20.1 feet.
Machinery: T.3-cyl. by the Shipbuilders.
History: 6.1886: Completed by Palmers Co.Ltd., Newcastle-upon-Tyne as *W.I.Radcliffe* for
W.I. Radcliffe S.S. Co.Ltd., Cardiff (Evan Thomas, Radcliffe & Co., managers). 1903:
Purchased by Aberporth S.S. Co.Ltd. (D. Jenkins & Co., managers) and re-named
Aberporth. 19.6.1905: Foundered in the Black Sea with a cargo of manganese ore, bound
from Poti to Antwerp.

Saint Regulus
In the Fleet: 1905-1907
Official No.: 93700
Tonnage Gross: 3131
Tonnage Nett: 1919
Length: 336.4 x Beam: 42.2 x Depth/Draught: 27.8 feet.
Machinery: T.3-cyl. by J. Jack & Co., Liverpool.
History: 8.1886: Completed by T. Royden & Sons, Liverpool for British & Foreign S.S. Co.
(Rankin, Gilmour & Co., Liverpool, managers). 1899: Sold to Sir Alfred Hickman S.S. Co.
(Eeles, Ruston & McMullen, Cardiff, managers). 1902: Transferred to Saint Regulus S.S. Co.
(same managers). 1905: Management transferred to D. Jenkins and S.R. Ruston, Cardiff.
1907: Management transferred to S.R. Ruston & Co., Cardiff. 1908: Broken up at Blyth.

Kingsland
In the Fleet: 1905-1910
Official No.: 119976
Tonnage Gross: 2831
Tonnage Nett: 1808
Length: 314.0 x Beam: 48.0 x Depth/Draught: 20.6 feet.
Machinery: T.3-cyl. by North Eastern Marine Engineering Co.Ltd., Sunderland.
History: 9.1905: Completed by Sunderland S.B. Co.Ltd., Sunderland for Kingsland S.S.
Co.Ltd. (D. Jenkins and S.R. Ruston, Cardiff, managers). 1907: Management transferred to
S.R. Ruston & Co., Cardiff. 1910: Management transferred to Philipps, Philipps & Co.Ltd.
1912: Purchased by Scottish S.S. Co.Ltd. and re-named *King Arthur*. 1913: Sold to
J.L. Mowinckel, Norway and re-named *Heina*. 1921: Sold to Reiersen & Matland, Norway
and re-named *Strudsholm*. 1921: Sold to M. Sato, Japan. 1922: Re-named *Atsuta Maru No.
1*. 27.8.1926: Wrecked at Tsuchizaki.

Ships' Masters, 1897-1927

(These details are based upon information taken from the Lloyd's Captains' Registers preserved at the Guildhall Library, London, Mss. 18567-18569. This list shows the regular commands of the various masters over specified periods, but does not include the relief turns that they or others undertook from time to time on the firms' vessels).

1. A. Balleine, Cardiff
   S.S.*Glamorgan* 1917-19

2. A. Chaplin, South Shields.
   S.S.*Farringford* 1900-03.

3. J. Davies, Aber-porth.
   S.S.*Rowtor* 1904-06,
   S.S.*Cardigan* (1) 1907-10,
   S.S.*Glamorgan* 1910-12.

4. T.L. Davies, Dinas Cross.
   S.S.*Farringford* 1911-14,
   S.S.*Glamorgan* 1915-17,
   S.S.*Huntshead* 1917-21,
   S.S.*Merioneth* (2) 1924-27.

5. E.T. Elias, Bethesda.
   S.S.*North Tyne* 1900,
   S.S.*Rowtor* 1901-03,
   S.S.*Farringford* 1904.

6. T. Evans, Cardigan.
   S.S.*Kingsland* 1905-10.

7. F.F. Foley, Aberafan.
   S.S.*Farringford* 1915-16.

8. T. Herbert.
   S.S.*North Tyne* 1898-99.

9. J.H. James, Aber-porth.
   S.S.*Gathorne* 1899, S.S.*Powis* 1900.

10. Daniel Jenkins, Aber-porth, later of Tre-saith.
    S.S.*Powis* 1902, S.S.*Rowtor* 1903,
    S.S.*Straits of Menai* 1903-04,
    S.S.*Italiana* 1905, S.S.*Glamorgan* 1906-07.

11. David Jenkins, Aber-porth.
    S.S.*Straits of Menai* 1900-02,
    S.S.*Italiana* 1903-04,
    S.S.*Farringford* 1904-10,
    S.S.*Cardigan* (1) 1910-11.

12. D. Jones, Cardigan.
    S.S.*Powis* 1899.

13. D.R. Jones, Caernarfon.
    S.S.*Merioneth* (1) 1916-17.

14. H. Jones, Nefyn.
    S.S.*Italiana* 1905-07,
    S.S.*Glamorgan* 1908-1910.

15. J.P. Jones, Beulah, Cardigan.
    S.S.*Italiana* 1911-12,
    S.S.*Glamorgan* 1912-14.

16. W. Jones, Borth.
    S.S.*North Tyne* 1900-04.

17. W. Jones, Caernarfon.
    S.S.*North Tyne* 1898, S.S.*Powis* 1899, S.S.*Rowtor* 1900.

18. W. Lauritson, Cardiff.
    S.S.*Anglesea* (2) 1917,
    S.S.*Daghild* 1917, S.S.*Anglesea* (2) 1918-21.

19. J. Lloyd, Borth.
    S.S.*Saint Regulus* 1905-07.

20. J.M. Lloyd, Conwy.
    S.S.*Italiana* 1902, S.S.*Powis* 1904.

21. J. McLaren, Glasgow.
    S.S.*Italiana* 1913.

22. J. Phillips, Haverfordwest.
    S.S.*Rowtor* 1898-99, S.S.*North Tyne* 1899, S.S.*Italiana* 1900-01,
    S.S.*Powis* 1905-07.

23. G. Pritchard, Pwllheli.
    S.S.*Powis* 1901.

24. E.M. Roberts, Cricieth.
    S.S.*Farringford* 1913,
    S.S.*Glamorgan* 1914.

25. G. Roberts, Pwllheli.
S.S.*Italiana* 1914-15,
S.S.*Merioneth* (1) 1916,
S.S.*Carmarthen* 1916-17.

26. H. Roberts, Nefyn.
S.S.*Aberporth* 1903, S.S.*Italiana*
1916.

27. W. Roberts, Cricieth.
S.S.*Gathorne* 1900.

28. T. Sullivan, Cardiff.
S.S.*Italiana* 1907.

29. S. Thomas, Aber-porth.
S.S.*Gathorne* 1897-98,
S.S.*Aberporth* 1905.

30. J.O. Wilkinson, Sunderland.
S.S.*Aberporth* 1904-05.

31. H. Williamson, Cardiff, later of
St. Dogmaels.
S.S.*Italiana* 1908-10,
S.S.*Cardigan* (1) 1911-14,
S.S.*Anglesea* (1) 1914-17,
S.S.*Cardigan* (2) 1917-21,
S.S.*Anglesea* (2) 1922,
S.S.*Radnor* 1923-27.

32. ? Woodhall.
S.S.*Gathorne* 1901.

Crew Lists

(The lists for 1904 and 1905 have been taken from the 10% sample at the National Maritime Museum; the remainder are from the archives of the Maritime History Group of the Memorial University of St. Johns, Newfoundland, Canada).

Crew of S.S.*Rowtor*
Signed-on at Barry, 22 August 1905   age

John Davies, Aber-porth, master	33
R.R. Morris, Bryncir, 1st mate	34
Griffith Thomas, Aber-porth, 2nd mate	23
D.E. Arnold, Cardiff, steward	29
J. Evans, Cardiff, cook	25
R. Jones, Cardiff, master's steward	19
R. Hume, Dunbar, bosun	35
D. Browne, Cardiff, A.B.	17
A. Pedrera, Cardiff (Spanish), A.B.	23
R. Campela, Cardiff (Spanish), A.B.	32
S. Variego, Cardiff (Spanish), A.B.	27
M. Jones, Newcastle Emlyn, O.S.	16
H. Shorter, Penarth, O.S.	16
F. Phillips, Cardiff, 1st engineer	30
R.O. Thomas, Bethesda, 2nd engineer	25
T. Dent, Cardiff, 3rd engineer	29
G. Julio, Cardiff (Greek), donkeyman	21
J. Messier, Cardiff (French), fireman	33
A. Balio, Cardiff (Spanish), fireman	43
T. O'Hara, Liverpool (Irish), fireman	34
B. Beretich, Cardiff (Hungarian), fireman	25

Crew of S.S.*Powis*
Signed-on at Penarth, 12 September 1905

J. Phillips, Haverfordwest, master	39
J.G. Davies, Rhydlewis, 1st mate	42
John Evans, Cilgerran, 2nd mate	52
E. Rees, Aber-porth, steward	46
A. Hollins, Cardiff, cook	40
E. Dwyer, Cardiff, master's steward	15
W. Pryce, Solfach, bosun	29
W.B. Jenkins, Solfach, A.B.	20
F. Fernall, Cardiff, A.B.	32
A. Perez, Cardiff (Spanish), A.B.	24
V. Viceta, Cardiff (Spanish), A.B.	27
E. Andrews, Cardiff, O.S.	24
J. Garrett, Barry, 1st engineer	26
D.J. Davies, Dinas Cross, 2nd engineer	21
J. Reed, Barry Dock, 3rd engineer	29
S. Harding, Cardiff, donkeyman	45
C. de Vito, Cardiff (Spanish), fireman	37
A. Rodriguez, Cardiff (Spanish), fireman	29
J. Doze, Cardiff (Spanish), fireman	23
J. Sanchez, Cardiff (Spanish), fireman	33

Crew of S.S. *Straits of Menai*
Signed-on at Barry, 2 November 1904   age

E.T. Elias, Bethesda, master	33
D. Davies, Newport Pembs., 1st mate	48
D.J. Evans, Llanon, 2nd mate	23
J. Roberts, Cricieth, steward	45
A. Pearce, London, cook	31
E. Wilson, West Hartlepool, captain's steward	16
L.H. Lammy, Cardiff, bosun	22
P. Borgitos, Cardiff (Greek), A.B.	35
G. Arnold, Cardiff, A.B.	49
W. Fitzgerald, London, A.B.	43
James Lucas, Cardiff, A.B.	30
James Gillespie, Cardiff, A.B.	26
Lucas Kerz, Cardiff (German), A.B.	32
W. Brown, Cardiff, 1st engineer	44
A. Davies, Cardiff, 2nd engineer	30
A. Hemmingway, Cardiff, 3rd engineer	23
M. Giovanni, Cardiff (Italian), donkeyman	25
H.J. Edward, Cardiff, fireman	25
H. Rogers, Cardiff, fireman	24
A. Dunovich, Cardiff (Hungarian), fireman	26
T. Morrison, Cardiff, fireman	26
E. Kinney, Cardiff (Irish), fireman	38

Crew of S.S. *Farringford*
Signed-on at Barry, 24 November 1904

David Jenkins, Aber-porth, master	47
J. Lewis, Llangrannog, 1st mate	30
J. Chapman, Swansea, 2nd mate	30
W. Taverna, Cardiff (Greek), steward	48
F. Harrison, Barry, cook	31
A.J. Taralla, Cardiff (Turkish), master's steward	22
A. Galiana, Cardiff (Turkish), carpenter	43
J.O. Evans, Aber-porth, bosun	26
G. Davies, Aber-porth, A.B.	19
P. Vargas, Cardiff (Spanish), A.B.	31
A. Bonero, Cardiff (Mexican), A.B.	22
M. Frances, Cardiff (Spanish), A.B.	32
S. Evans, Ferndale, O.S.	17
T. Venables, Cardiff, 1st engineer	34
T.J. Davies, Newport Mon., 2nd engineer	29
T.J. Thomas, Bangor, 3rd engineer	25
José Iora, Cardiff (Spanish), donkeyman	23
M. Nabarto, Cardiff (Spanish), fireman	27
A. Falas, Cardiff (Spanish), fireman	27
A. Jose, Cardiff (Spanish), fireman	41
P. Gerado, Cardiff (Spanish), fireman	51

Crew of S.S. *Italiana*
Signed-on at Barry, 6 May 1905

Daniel Jenkins, Tre-saith, master	34
Hugh Jones, Nefyn, 1st mate	39
R. Jones, Aberaeron, 2nd mate	29

G. Halloran, Cardiff, steward	28
E. Walcott, Cardiff, cook	38
W.D. Helsop, Bristol, master's steward	18
T.M. Thomas, Aber-porth, bosun	28
J. Davies, Aber-porth, A.B.	18
J. Owens, Aber-porth, A.B.	18
G. Parry, Bridgend, A.B.	19
A. Campbell, Cardiff (Scot.), A.B.	23
L. Joseph, Cardiff, A.B.	27
V. Torres, Cardiff (Spanish), A.B.	37
E.W. Cooke, Newport Mon., 1st engineer	36
E.R. Roberts, Holyhead, 2nd engineer	24
W.N. Lewis, Moylgrove, 3rd engineer	21
S. Bryant, Cardiff, donkeyman	29
R. Roman, Cardiff (Portugese), fireman	32
J. Olinos, Cardiff (Spanish), fireman	20
P. Passagotta, Cardiff (Spanish), fireman	34
B. Garcia, Cardiff (Spanish), fireman	45
J.R. Jenkins, Aber-porth, O.S.	17
J. Taylor, Glasgow, O.S.	31

Crew of S.S. *Farringford*
Signed-on at Barry, 2 March 1914

T.L. Davies, Dinas Cross, master	31
F. Foley, Aberafan, 1st mate	46
W.M. Evans, Aberaeron, 2nd mate	38
T.M. Thomas, Aber-porth, bosun	36
T.Ll. Davies, New Quay, A.B.	27
F.W. Hardwick, Barry, A.B.	20
M. Allen, Cardiff (Irish), O.S.	21
J. O'Leary, Cardiff (Irish), A.B.	23
M. McCarthy, Cardiff (Irish), A.B.	28
Joseph Leary, Cardiff (Irish), O.S.	21
J.L. James, Aber-porth, O.S.	15
S.R. Davies, Cwm-cou, 1st engineer	28
H. Vaughan, Cardiff, 2nd engineer	33
Thomas Meredith, Morriston, 3rd engineer	22
O. Negard, Cardiff (Norwegian), donkeyman	41
C. Isaac, Cardiff (St. Kitts), fireman	43
J.H. Johnson, Virginia U.S.A., fireman	38
R. Bechoras, Cardiff (Spanish), fireman	27
E. Aldominez, Cardiff (Spanish), fireman	46
A. Hernacles, London (Greek), fireman	23
C.A. Carlson, Cardiff (Swedish), fireman	32
E. Rees, Aber-porth, steward	53
John J. Rees, Aber-porth, master's steward	15
T. Vautier, Southampton, cook	50

Crew of S.S. *Glamorgan*
Signed-on at Barry, 10 September 1914

J.P. Jones, Beulah, master	47
G. Davies, Aber-porth, 1st mate	27

	age
R. Lloyd, Nefyn, 2nd mate	28
John Williams, Porthmadog, bosun	46
Albert Richards, Aberdyfi, A.B.	35
D. Morris, Cardigan, O.S.	21
W. Morris, St. Dogmaels, O.S.	23
K. Trykina, Cardiff (Norwegian), A.B.	27
E. Martinsen, Cardiff (Norwegian), O.S.	25
F. Chagnon, Aber-porth, O.S.	15
Isaac Evans, Llanon, O.S.	18
Thomas Venables, South Shields, 1st engineer	44
D. Francis, Dinas Cross, 2nd engineer	31
E. Hooton, Llandaff, 3rd engineer	25
G. Davies, Penarth, 4th engineer	21
J. Hastie, Blyth, donkeyman	40
C. Libante, Cardiff (St. Kitts), fireman	23
W. Packling, Cardiff (St. Kitts), fireman	27
W. Henry, Cardiff (Bermuda), fireman	29
R. Dulcie, Cardiff (Santa Lucia), fireman	21
J. Griffith, Cardiff (Barbados), fireman	30
M. Lynch, Cardiff (Santa Lucia), fireman	29
J. Thomas, Barry, fireman	25
G. Kent, North Shields, steward	50
F.W. Blythe, Talywain, master's steward	20
N. Campbell, Belfast, cook	37
K. Olafsen, Cardiff (Norwegian), A.B.	45

Crew of S.S. *Cardigan*
Signed-on at Penarth, 25 November 1913

	age
H. Williamson, Cardiff, master	32
G. Roberts, Pwllheli, 1st mate	40
W.R. Williams, Caernarfon, 2nd mate	30
R.W. Jones, Cardiff, steward	53
A. Oeven, Amsterdam, cook	37
H.C. Vos, Amsterdam, master's steward	26
E.R. Roberts, Holyhead, 1st engineer	32
T.P. Salmon, Cardiff, 2nd engineer	39
W.J. Thomas, Treorchy, 3rd engineer	23
W.C. Lewis, Barry, 4th engineer	26
J. Davies, Aber-porth, bosun	41
J. O'Neill, Dublin, A.B.	24
J. Porter, Dublin, A.B.	23
W. Davies, Rhiw, O.S.	20
J. Browne, Dublin, O.S.	22
W. Harding, Belfast, A.B.	24
G. Smith, Aber-porth, O.S.	20
J. Evans, Cardiff, A.B.	52
James Evans, Blaenporth, O.S.	22
D. Morris, Cardigan, O.S.	19
W. Brimblecombe, Cardiff, donkeyman	49
M. Jones, Cardiff, fireman	28
T. Lomprer, South Shields, fireman	48
C. Holder, Cardiff (Barbados), fireman	33
T. Pickett. Dublin, fireman	34

B. Thomas, Cardiff, fireman	33
T. Driscoll, Cardiff, fireman	33
O. Johannessen, Cardiff (Swedish), fireman	26
F. Vera, Cardiff (Mauritius), fireman	27

Crew of S.S. *Anglesea*
Signed-on at Stockton-on-Tees, 13 July 1914

H. Williamson, Cardiff, master	33
J.R. Davies, Aberaeron, 1st mate	40
W. Griffiths, Porthmadog, 2nd mate	41
L. Williams, Porthmadog, steward	26
R.J. Owen, Porthmadog, cook	49
C.H. Rennison, Hull, master's steward	24
H. Winder, Stockton, carpenter	25
David Rees, St. Dogmaels, bosun	35
James Watt, Lerwick, A.B.	33
P. Nielsen, North Shields, A.B.	34
P. Queen, Leith, A.B.	52
G. Wannell, Stockton, A.B.	32
E. Powson, Harrogate, A.B.	33
M. Hartshund, Middlesborough (Norwegian), A.B.	55
S.R. Davies, Cwm-cou, 1st engineer	29
R.J. Bennett, Barry, 2nd engineer	26
John Davies, Cardigan, 3rd engineer	26
George Perry, Bradford, 4th engineer	23
W.H. Hastings, Stockton, donkeyman	42
P. Loughran, Consett, fireman	32
W. Cunningham, Middlesborough, fireman	36
W. Parks, Middlesborough, fireman	24
J.L. Thompson, Stockton, fireman	58
P. Coleman, Middlesborough, fireman	23
T. Cosgrave, Cardiff (Irish), fireman	32
T. Davies, Cwmtwrch, fireman	38
J. Robins, Bristol, fireman	43
O.L. Jenkins, Newquay, O.S.	15
E.O. Jenkins, Aber-porth, O.S.	15
C. Humphreys, Barry, O.S.	21

Crew of S.S. *Italiana*
Signed-on at Barry, 25 May 1916

Hugh Roberts, Nefyn, master	62
D.J. Evans, Llanon, 1st mate	30
R.G. Davies, Fishguard, 2nd mate	52
W. Parker, Barry, bosun	42
J. Manning, London, O.S.	22
J. Burns, Penarth, A.B.	34
G.T. Lewis, Aberaeron, O.S.	23
Jenkin Evans, Llanon, A.B.	44
G. Gregory, Plymouth, O.S.	26
L. John, Barry, O.S.	22
John Brown, Aber-porth, O.S.	16
John Sampson, Liverpool, 1st engineer	57

C. Griffiths, Pontnewydd, 2nd engineer   32
W.D. Jones, Swansea, 3rd engineer   36
S. Harding, Cardiff, donkeyman   57
Abdulla Mahomed, Cardiff (Arab), fireman   29
Abdul Assis, Cardiff (Arab), fireman   36
Nasir Ali, Cardiff (Arab), fireman   29
Ralmin Nahli, Cardiff (Arab), fireman   21
Abdullah Mohamed, Cardiff (Arab), fireman   22
Jaheh Ahmed, Cardiff (Arab), fireman   21
William Jones, Borth, steward   25
W.S. Seed, Swansea, cook   26
D.J. Gray, Cardigan, master's steward   15

Crew of S.S.*Radnor*
Signed-on at Middlesborough, 9 August 1923

H. Williamson, Cardiff, master   42
A. Balleine, Cardiff, 1st mate   43
E.O. Jenkins, Aber-porth, 2nd mate   23
T.H. Davies, Aber-porth, 3rd mate   25
H. Outhwaite, Stockton-on-Tees, carpenter   25
T. Beard, Gloucester, bosun   38
S. Carr, Middlesborough, A.B.   25
J. Gatenby, Middlesborough, A.B.   23
A. Wright, Middlesborough, A.B.   24
N. Roll, Whitby, O.S.   20
H. Jack, ?, O.S.   20
A. Sartoris, Cardiff (Chilean), O.S.   27
S.R. Davies, Cwm-cou, 1st engineer   38
W.G. Stephens, Stockton-on-Tees, 2nd engineer   54
H. Lobb, Stockton-on-Tees, 3rd engineer   31
D. Bearley, Stockton-on-Tees, 4th engineer   21
J. Roper, Middlesborough, donkeyman   47
T. Cutler, Glasgow, fireman   26
P. McGarth, Middlesborough, fireman   24
J. McDonald, Middlesborough, fireman   47
T. Allen, West Hartlepool, fireman   28
I. Dodds, Stockton-on-Tees, fireman   52
E. Shepherd, Cardiff, fireman   33
M. Turley, Middlesborough, fireman   26
T. Metcalfe, Haverton Hill, fireman   33
J. Ord, Middlesborough, fireman   52
J. Moon, Middlesborough, fireman   32
G. Nash, Cheltenham, steward   55
J. Williams, Sarnau, Cardigan, master's steward   15
T.L. Perriman, Barry, cook   22
J. Morgan, Cenarth, galley boy   20
Evan Jones, Blaenannerch, Cardigan, cabin boy   18
J.H. Mansfield, Glasgow, wireless operator   27

Crew of S.S.*Merioneth*
Signed-on at Barry, 25 May 1924

T.L. Davies, Dinas Cross, master   41
R. Lloyd, Nefyn, 1st mate   37

E.O. Jenkins, Aber-porth, 2nd mate	24
T.E. James, Aber-porth, 3rd mate	23
C. Cambarakis, Cardiff (Greek), bosun	38
H. Birks, West Hartlepool, carpenter	30
D. Thomas, Aber-porth, A.B.	38
L.J. Herbert, Borth, A.B.	28
H. Griffiths, Nefyn, O.S.	20
J. Jones, Rhydlewis, A.B.	32
D.L. Jones, Cardigan, O.S.	23
L.G. Jones, Llangrannog, O.S.	23
J. Nixon, West Hartlepool, 1st engineer	32
D.G. Williams, St. Dogmaels, 2nd engineer	36
W. Taylor, West Hartlepool, 3rd engineer	34
W.S. Pallett, West Hartlepool, 4th engineer	24
I. Tontanallis, Cardiff (Spanish), donkeyman	41
J. Stanley, Liverpool, fireman	20
W. Harries, Barry, fireman	38
J. Ramsey, Cardiff, fireman	49
J.T. Oram, Barry, fireman	23
T.C. Forman, Cardiff, fireman	27
T.J. Savage, Waterford, fireman	46
A. Sapade, Cardiff (Maltese), fireman	47
J. MacKinnon, Isle of Barra, fireman	20
P.J. Cronin, Barry, fireman	21
C. Olsen, Cardiff (Danish), fireman	53
T.H. Brayley, Cardiff, steward	32
D.O. Powell, Aberystwyth, cabin boy	19
F.G. Good, Harwich, cook	29
W.C. James, Tremain, Cardigan, galley boy	15
H.E. Stather, West Hartlepool, master's steward	17
P.J. O'Keeffe, Skibbereen, wireless operator	24

The Prospectus of
The 'Cardigan' Steamship Company, Ltd.

Registered Office: MERCHANTS' EXCHANGE CARDIFF

Dear Sir or Madam,

We have great pleasure in placing before you particulars of a Steamer contracted for in October last for delivery in June/July next, strikes, etc., excepted. The Steamer will be named the 'CARDIGAN', and will carry about 7,100 tons dead weight on 23ft. 4in. draft.

By contracting for this Steamer at the above time, we secured one of the cheapest vessels ever built. Since then Building Material has advanced considerably, and we could not now duplicate this vessel except at an appreciably higher figure. Every keen investor knows that the best time to buy is when Building Material is low, and we consider we have taken advantage of this opportunity in securing the present contract.

In arranging the plans and specifications, we have introduced all the latest improvements, and annexed we give particulars. It will be seen by those who are aquainted with Shipping Properties that the Steamer will be one of the best equipped vessels for trading purposes, as well as one of the cheapest. We cannot too strongly draw your attention to this, as it stands to reason that ships that are not fully equipped in the beginning cannot be as successful in the long run as their superior rivals.

The Steamer is being built and engined by the eminent firms of Messrs. R. Ropner & Son, Stockton-on-Tees, and Messrs. The North Eastern Marine Engineering Co.Ltd., of Sunderland, respectively. The Steamer will be built under special survey on the famous 'Trunk' system, and will take the highest Class in the British Corporation Registry, which will enable her to be insured at the lowest possible rates at Lloyds. This type of Steamer is well arranged and admirably equipped for the rapid handling of all cargoes. Moreover, the trimming charges on coal cargoes will be on a modified scale, thus affording a considerable saving. The Steamer possesses other advantages over the ordinary type, such as low register tonnage (on which port dues are levied), and owing to excellent cubic capacity will be well adapted for carrying light cargoes.

The Contract price of £39,930 is inclusive of all extras and improvements over the usual Shipbuilders' specifications.

No intermediate profit or commission of any kind is being made, the Steamer with all the benefits of the Contract being transferred to the Company at identically the same cost.

The cost of this vessel works out at the remarkably low price of £5 12s. 6d. per ton, thus making her, as above stated, one of the cheapest vessels ever built, and we may here remark that we have gone in for larger Engines than the majority of tramp steamers at an extra cost of £730. These Engines will be capable of driving the vessel fully laden about 10 knots per hour in moderate weather. This as you may imagine is an important factor, and will enable her to make quicker passages, thereby placing her at an advantage over the majority of cargo steamers.

The nominal Capital of the Company is £35,000, divided into 350 Shares of £100 each, and the Company has been incorporated under the Companies' Acts, 1862 to 1900, as the 'Cardigan' Steamship Company, Limited.

The liability of each Shareholder is absolutely limited to the number of Shares allotted.

The balance of £4,930 will be discharged by the creation of a Sinking Fund. By adopting this principle the Shares should maintain their original value, and by the time this amount has been paid off, the cost of the vessel will be reduced. Moreover, this method will give fewer Shareholders to divide the profits between.

The minimum subscription upon which the Directors may proceed to Allotment is £8,000.

The Shares are payable as follows:-

    £5 per Share on application.
    £95   ''   ''   June 30th, 1907.

but if any applicant prefers, the Directors may receive payments as follows:-

    £5 0 0 per Share on Application.
    £45 0 0   ''   ''   June 30th, 1907.
    £10 0 0   ''   ''   December 31st, 1907.
    £10 0 0   ''   ''   June 30th, 1908.
    £10 0 0   ''   ''   December 31st, 1908.
    £10 0 0   ''   ''   June 30th, 1909.
    £10 0 0   ''   ''   December 31st, 1909.

Any Shareholder desiring to pay according to the latter terms will be charged 5 per cent interest per annum on the last five instalments only, viz., from 30th June, 1907, to the actual date of payment, but will receive dividends upon Shares with other Shareholders as if their Shares were fully paid on the 30th June, 1907.

The preliminary and formation expenses are estimated at £1,000, and will be paid by the Company.

The Secretarial work will be performed free of expense to the Company, the cost being borne by the Directors and Managers.

The Steamer will be fully insured against every possible contingency and risk, making the investment perfectly secure.

The Directors and Managers of the Company will be James Jenkins and David Jenkins, both of Merchants' Exchange, Cardiff, trading as Jenkins Brothers.

The remuneration of the Directors and Managers will be 2½ per cent on the gross earnings of the Steamer, or 5 per cent on chartered freight when the vessel is on Time Charter, together with the usual fees received for acting as Shipbrokers when such are payable.

A copy of the Memorandum of Association of the Company will be seen in the fold of this Prospectus.

The Company may exercise the power conferred by Section 8 of the Companies Act, 1900, to pay a commission not exceeding 2½ per cent on any Shares offered to the public for subscription.

The Auditor of the Company will be appointed in accordance with Section 21 of the Companies Act, 1900.

The following are the only Contracts that have been entered into:-

Contract for the construction of the Steamer at £39,930, dated the 31st day of October, 1906, made between Messrs. R. Ropner and Son, Shipbuilders, of Stockton-on-Tees, of the one part, and Jenkins Brothers, Shipowners, of Merchants' Exchange, Cardiff, of the other part.

Agreement dated March 26th, 1907, between James Jenkins and David Jenkins of the one part, and the Company of the other part, whereby the said James Jenkins and David Jenkins re-sell to the Company the Steamer at the same figure, and the said James Jenkins and David Jenkins are appointed Managers of the Steamer.

The above Agreements, together with copies of the Memorandum and Articles of Association, can be inspected at the Office of the Company during ordinary business hours.

Should no Allotment of Shares be made, the moneys received on Application will be returned in full.

Enclosed is a Form of Application for Shares, which should be filled in and returned to the Registered Office of the Company, Merchants' Exchange, Cardiff, or to the Company's Bankers, The London and Provincial Bank, Limited, Barry, Glam., who will be glad to answer any inquiry you may wish respecting our firm.

If required, further Prospectuses and Forms of Application can be obtained at the Office of the Company or from the Bankers.

Any further information you may require we shall be pleased to furnish, as we desire and solicit the fullest possible inquiry. We candidly believe this investment is one of the best ever placed before the public, and as such we have no hesitation in recommending same.

Yours faithfully,

Jenkins Bros.

Cardiff, April 8th, 1907.

PARTICULARS OF S.S. 'CARDIGAN'.

Built under Special Survey to the highest class of the British Corporation Registry.
Length between perpendiculars, 355ft. Breadth, 51ft. Depth moulded, 28ft. 5in.
Draft loaded, 23ft. 4in.
Hull and Machinery specially designed to full and complete Specification for successful and economical working in all trades.
Large Donkey Boiler, 10ft. by 10ft., 100lbs. pressure.
15 Ton Evaporator and Feed Heater.
Propeller Shaft with continuous brass liner.
Steam Ash Hoist.
Air Pump of the Edwards' Patent Type.
Triple Expansion Engine, 25 by 42½ by 69 with 48in. stroke.
Two Large Single-ended Boilers, 16ft. 6in. by 11ft. 6in., 180lbs. pressure, fitted with Morrison's Patent Suspension Furnaces.
Smoke boxes fitted with Silley's patent air-tight doors.
Boilers raised 2ft. 6in. above tank top.
Telescopic Masts.

Six Steel Bulkheads.

Six Powerful Steam Winches, 7in. by 12in , with bronze piston and valve rods. The winches exhaust back to tank in Engine Room.

Emmerson and Walker's Direct Steam Windlass of the latest type with quick warping ends.

Rodger's Steam Steering Gear.

Improved Steam Starting and Reversing Engine.

Two Patent Repeating Telegraphs and speaking tube from Bridge to Engine Room.

Byers' Patent Anchors.

Lord Kelvin's Compass.

Plate Keel and Bilge Keels.

Single Plate Rudder. Suez Canal Rudder.

Shifting Boards, fitted to comply with Board of Trade Grain Act.

Ample Water Ballast in Cellular Double Bottom (none under Boilers).

Fresh Water Tanks for 4,000 Gallons.

Large Hatchways for quick loading and discharging of cargo.

Cargo Gangways and Special Platforms abreast of each hatchway to facilitate quick handling of cargo.

Recess for Spare Tail end Shaft in Tunnel.

Spare Propeller.

Spare Tail end Shaft.

Iron Bulkhead between Engines and Boilers.

Engine and Boiler casing 7ft. 3in. high.

Four Donkey Pumps.

One spare set of main and donkey fire bars, valves, and other necessary spare gear.

Spacious accommodation for Captain, Officers and Engineers on bridge deck. Crew in forecastle.

Vessel fitted with full and complete working outfit.

References

The following abbreviations have been used:
N.L.W. - National Library of Wales, Aberystwyth.
P.R.O. - Public Record Office, Kew, London.
W.I.M.M. - Welsh Industrial and Maritime Museum

Chapter 1

1. Jenkins, J. Geraint, 'Herring Fishing in Wales', *Maritime Wales*, No. 4 (1979), pp.5-32.
2. Jenkins, J. Geraint, *Maritime Heritage - The Ships and Seamen of Southern Ceredigion* (Llandysul, 1982), p.84.
3. *ibid.*, p.113.
4. P.R.O., B.T. 31/2397/11955.
5. Shipping registers of the Port of Cardigan, H.M. Customs and Excise, Fishguard Harbour.
6. Dyfed Archives (Haverfordwest Office), log books and crew agreements of the smack *Mary Jane*, 1868-1893, (T/RS).
7. Shipping registers of the Port of Cardigan, H.M. Customs and Excise, Fishguard Harbour.
8. Jenkins, David, *Hanes yr Hen Gapel yn Aber-porth* (1983), p.21.
9. Jenkins, J. Geraint, *op.cit.*, (1982), p.86.
10. Dyfed Archives, log books and crew agreements of the ketch *James*, 1890-1910, (T/RS).
11. Personal recollections, Mr. Frank Chagnon, Aber-porth.
12. Personal recollections, the late Mrs. Grace Jenkins, Aber-porth.

Chapter 2

1. Jenkins, J. Geraint, *Evan Thomas, Radcliffe: a Cardiff Shipping Company* (Cardiff, 1982).
2. Craig, R., 'Trade and Shipping in South Wales - the Radcliffe Company, 1882-1921'. (To be published by the University of Wales Press).
3. The details regarding the vessels commanded by James and David Jenkins have been taken from Lloyd's Captains' Registers, now deposited at the Guildhall Library, London (Ms. series 18567, 18568, 18569).
4. See Chapter 1, note 8.
5. Craig, R., *op.cit.*
6. Daunton, M.J., *Coal Metropolis: Cardiff, 1870-1914* (Leicester, 1977), pp.64,65. Craig, R., *The Ship: Steam Tramps and Cargo Liners, 1850-1950* (H.M.S.O., 1980), p.42.
7. Hill, J.C.G., *Shipshape and Bristol Fashion* (Liverpool, n.d.), pp.35,96.
8. P.R.O., B.T.31/7200/50904.
9. Obituaries in *South Wales Daily News* 30 June 1913 and *Barry Dock News* 4 July 1913.
10. Craig, R., *op.cit.*, (1980), pp.11-17, 31-37.
11. P.R.O., B.T.31/7844/56147.

Chapter 3

1. Craig, R., *The Ship: Steam Tramps and Cargo Liners 1850-1950* (HMSO, 1980), p.39.
2. Green, E. and Moss, M., *A Business of National Importance: The Royal Mail Shipping Group, 1902-1937* (London, 1982), p.14.
3. P.R.O., B.T.31/16085/59619.

4. P.R.O., B.T.31/16113/60160.
5. P.R.O., B.T.31/8825/64763.
6. I am indebted to Mr. Robin Craig for this reference.
7. P.R.O., B.T.31/16499/67675.
8. P.R.O., B.T.31/16519/67925.
9. *Maritime Review* Vol.1, No.2 (24 February 1904), p.42.
10. *ibid.*
11. Aldcroft, D.H., 'The Depression in British Shipping, 1901-11' in Aldcroft, D.H., *Studies in British Transport History, 1870-1970* (Newton Abbot, 1974), p.100.
12. *Western Mail* 29 April 1901.
13. These details and those quotes which follow are taken from Captain Jenkins' letter book in the possession of his son, Captain D.O. Jenkins, Swansea, pp. 112-228.
14. *Maritime Review* Vol.II, No.16 (June 1 1904), p.69.
15. See note 5.
16. For the subsequent history of the company and T.H. Mordey's eventual bankruptcy, see the *Western Mail* 17 July 1931.

Chapter 4

1. *Western Mail Cardiff Directories*, 1897-1903.
2. Glamorgan Archives, CL. P/S. CBo. B.T.194.
3. *Cardiff Journal of Commerce* 29 July 1904, 17 January 1905.
4. Glamorgan Archives, CL. P/S. CBo. B.T.194.
5. *ibid.*
6. *Maritime Review* Vol.VII, No.82 (8 September 1905), p.78.
7. *Western Mail* 29 August 1905.
8. *Maritime Review* Vol.VII, No.82 (8 September 1905), p.78.
9. Glamorgan Archives, CL. P/S. CBo. B.T.194.
10. *Maritime Review* Vol.VII, No.83 (15 September 1905), p. 95.
11. Guildhall Library, London, Lloyds Captains' Registers, Ms.18567.
12. P.R.O., B.T.31/8532/62109.
13. P.R.O., B.T.31/9045/66895.
14. *Maritime Review* Vol.VII, No.82 (8 September 1905), p.67.
15. *Syren and Shipping* 18 October 1905, p.217. I am indebted to Mr. Robin Craig for this reference and to my colleague Bill Jones for details relating to F.H. Kirkhouse.
16. *Maritime Review* Vol.VIII, No.94 (1 December 1905), p.48 and Vol.VIII, No. 101 (19 January 1906), p.178.
17. Davies, J. Ifor, *Growing Up Among Sailors* (Gwynedd Archives Service, 1983), p.44 and *Western Mail* 20 August 1906 and 28 August 1906. I am indebted to my colleague Tom Sharpe of the Geology Department for the seismographic details of the Valparaiso earthquake.
18. Glamorgan Archives, D/D. Com/C.3.
19. See note 13; also Glamorgan Archives D/D. PRO/RBS. C1/8.

Chapter 5

1. Sturmey, G.K., *British Shipping and World Competition* (London, 1962), p.25.
2. Aldcroft, D.H., 'The Depression in British Shipping, 1901-11' in Aldcroft, D.H., *Studies in British Transport History, 1870-1970* (Newton Abbot, 1974), p.100.
3. Sturmey, G.K., *op.cit.* (1962), pp.34,35.
4. Glamorgan Archives CL. P/S. CBo. B.T.213.
5. Glamorgan Archives CL. P/S. CBo. B.T.207.
6. *ibid.*
7. Shipping Registers of the Port of Cardiff, H.M. Customs and Excise, Cardiff.
8. Craig, R., *The Ship: Steam Tramps and Cargo Liners, 1850-1950* (H.M.S.O., 1980), pp.35-37.

9. P.R.O., B.T.31/18044/92676.
10. Colyer, R.J., 'The Pryse Family of Gogerddan and the decline of a great estate, 1800-1960', *Welsh History Review* Vol.9, No.4, (December 1979), pp.415-417.
11. See note 4.
12. *ibid.*
13. *Western Mail* 10 August 1907.
14. See note 4.
15. See note 4.
16. See note 4.
17. See note 4.
18. *Syren and Shipping* 28 August 1907, p.223; 25 September 1907, p.327. *Maritime Review* Vol.XV, No.186 (6 September 1907), pp.56-58. I am indebted to Mr. Robin Craig for the reference from *Syren and Shipping*.
19. *Maritime Review* Vol.XIX, No.240 (19 September 1908), p.108.
20. P.R.O., B.T.31/16499/67675.

Chapter 6

1. This paragraph is based upon a passage from Jenkins, David, 'Aber-porth' in Davies and Rees (eds.), *Welsh Rural Communities* (Cardiff, 1960), pp.23, 24.
2. Jenkins, David, *op.cit.*, (1960), p.7.
3. Jenkins, J. Geraint, 'Herring Fishing in Wales', *Maritime Wales*, No.4 (1979), p.17.
4. Personal recollections, Captain D.O. Jenkins, Swansea.
5. Eames, Aled, *Machlud Hwyliau'r Cymry: The Twilight of Welsh Sail* (Cardiff, 1984), p.21.
6. These details are taken from Captain Thomas's note books, now in the possession of his nephew, Captain Roy Jenkins, Aber-porth.
7. Personal recollections, the late Captain Samuel Jenkins, Aber-porth.
8. *Western Mail*, 24 February 1940.
9. Personal recollections, Mr. Frank Chagnon, Aber-porth.
10. Lloyd's Captains' Registers, Guildhall Library, London, alsc personal recollections, Mr. J.M. Griffith, Rhoslan.
11. See note 7.
12. *Western Mail*, 12 August 1907.
13. See note 9.
14. Jenkins, David, *Hanes yr Hen Gapel yn Aber-porth* (1983), p.22.
15. See note 9.
16. Captain Daniel Jenkins's letter book, pp.310, 311.
17. *ibid.*, p.33.
18. See note 7.
19. Quoted in Hay, D., *War under the Red Ensign* (London, 1982), p.15.
20. W.I.M.M. accession 81.44.
21. Captain Daniel Jenkins's letter book, p.325.

Chapter 7

1. Taylor, A.J.P., *English History, 1914-1945* (Pelican, 1970 edition), pp.98,99.
2. Burrell, David, 'A tale of 20th century merchant venturers', *Lloyd's List* 19 January 1984, p.7.
3. Hay, D., *War under the Red Ensign* (London, 1982), p.11.
4. Fayle, D.E., *The War and the Shipping Industry* (Oxford, 1927), pp.151-153.
5. *ibid.*, p.164.
6. Crew lists of S.S.*Cardigan*, 1914; Maritime History Group of the Memorial University of St. Johns, Newfoundland.
7. Personal recollections, Mr. Frank Chagnon, Aber-porth.

8. Craig, R., 'Trade and Shipping in South Wales - the Radcliffe Company, 1881-1921'. (To be published by the University of Wales Press).
9. *Cardiff and South Wales Journal of Commerce* 15 June 1917, p.6.; P.R.O. B.T. 31/16085/59619. I am indebted to Mr. David Burrell for this reference.
10. Boswell, J.S. and Johns, B.R., 'Patriots or Profiteers? British Businessmen and the First World War', *Journal of European Economic History* Vol.XI No.2 (1982), pp.426,427.
11. I am indebted to Mr. Robin Craig for details relating to the William Gray Yard contracts.
12. Anon., 'Cardiff: Shipping and Shipowning', in *Cardiff 1921* (*Syren and Shipping* London 1921), p.47.
13. Records of the Cardigan Shipping Co. (190861), Companies' House, Cardiff.
14. Personal recollections, Mr. C.A. Roberts, Little Maplestead, Essex.
15. N.L.W., Calendars of Grants of Probate and Letters Administration, 1920.

Chapter 8

1. Personal recollections, Mr. D.B. Jenkins, Wraysbury and Mrs. N. Thomas, Ludlow.
2. Anon., 'Cardiff - Shipping and Shipowning' in *Cardiff 1921* (*Syren and Shipping*, London 1921), pp.51-53.
3. Morgan, K.O., *Rebirth of a Nation: Wales 1880-1980* (Oxford 1981), pp.212,213.
4. See, for instance, the report on the collapse of the Pennant Shipping Co., in the *Western Mail*, 26 August 1924.
5. See note 2.
6. I am indebted to Mr. Robin Craig for this reference.
7. *South Wales Journal of Commerce* 30 March 1920.
8. Personal recollections. Mr. E.J. Roberts, Sully.
9. Heaton, P.M., 'Graig Shipping: A Firm Foundation', *Sea Breezes* Vol.56, No.440 (August 1982), p.560.
10. Records of the Cardigan Shipping Co. (190861), Companies' House, Cardiff.
11. *Western Mail* 19, 25 April 1924.
12. See note 10.
13. See note 10.
14. Shipping registers of the Port of Cardiff, H.M. Customs and Excise, Cardiff.
15. Personal recollections, Mrs. N. Thomas, Ludlow.
16. *Western Mail* 12 July 1926.
17. *ibid.*, 17 November 1926.
18. *ibid.*, 13 July, 18 August 1927.